Internet Basics

without fear!

Internet Basics
without fear!

Quick-Start
Guide for Becoming
Internet-Friendly
In Just a Few Easy Steps

Revised Edition

by Shaun Fawcett, M.B.A.

Final Draft Publications, Montreal, Quebec, Canada

Cover: Pierre Lavallée, Seyabec Inc.
Printed and bound in Canada by AGMV-MARQUIS.

Canadian Cataloguing in Publication Data

Fawcett, Shaun, 1949-
Internet basics without fear: quick-start guide for becoming
Internet-friendly in just a few easy steps

Rev. ed.
Includes index.

ISBN 0-9684297-1-8

1. Internet (Computer network). I. Title
TK5105.875.I57F39 2000 004.67'8 C00-900108-5

Final Draft Publications
1501 Notre-Dame West, Suite No. 5
Montreal QC H3C 1L2
Canada

Quick Summary

Part 1 - Fear and the Internet

Chapters 1 through 3 cover the many of the fears, misgivings, trials and tribulations the author experienced as he became a more proficient Internet user over the years. He goes on to explain how he found most of the books about the Internet to be too technical in nature for non-technical people who just want to surf the Net and send and receive e-mail.

Part 2 - Overcoming the Fear

Chapter 4 explains and demystifies the Internet in concise and simple terms that can be grasped by just about anyone. In Chapter 5, the author defines and elaborates on his theory that a normal and natural fear of technology continues to keep many ordinary non-technical people from trying the Internet. He goes on to talk about the fears he faced personally while he worked to become Internet-friendly, and what he learned to help him overcome those fears.

Part 3 - Conquering the Internet

The heart of the Guide is Chapter 6, which contains all of the basics that a non-technical person needs to know to master the Internet, in eight easy steps. It starts with a no-nonsense explanation of the basic computer equipment and telephone connections required. It then goes on to cover topics ranging from, how to surf and search the Net to how to send and receive e-mails. It couldn't be explained much more simply.

Part 4 - Beyond the Basics

Chapter 7 is for users who want to use more advanced Internet capabilities. It provides a summary of the more challenging things that can be done on the Internet, from electronic discussion and live online chat groups, to how one can subscribe to and download Web pages, and then read them offline later.

Part 5 – Other Useful Information

Chapter 8 contains an eclectic alphabetical subject-index with over 100 researched Web addresses that demonstrate the diversity and power of the Internet. Chapter 9 is a brief glossary of more than 40 common Internet-related terms defined in plain English. Chapter 10 is a compilation of some lesser-known services and capabilities that can make the Internet experience more convenient and user-friendly. Finally, Chapter 11 answers some questions that are frequently asked about the Internet.

Table of Contents

Part 3: Conquering the Internet

Part 4: Beyond the Basics

Part 5: Other Useful Information

Preface

Before drafting the second edition of this guide I spent a few hours browsing around my local book superstore. It has an extensive collection of recent books relating both directly and indirectly to the Internet. My brief visit there once again confirmed my original decision to produce this "Internet guide for the ordinary person". That is to say, a person who simply wants to know how to "surf" the Internet and send and receive E-mails.

About 90% of the books I could find there were way over my head, and I have some technical background and knowledge. Not a lot, but after six years on the Internet, I would imagine a bit more than the average person, at least when it comes to basic uses of the Net. Most of those books were obviously written for relatively advanced Internet users. The remaining ones were more "beginner-type" books and reference manuals, "for the rest of us" as one of the best-selling publications claims to be. I also noticed a couple of other things during my bookstore tour.

For example, I continue to be amazed that there are numerous companies producing very thick volumes on the subject of the Internet that are simply compilations of Web site addresses. These same addresses of course, are fully available to anyone who has Internet access, just by doing a bit of keyword research using a Search Engine. As far as I can tell, these books are equivalent to someone reorganizing and then republishing the local phone directory, but with a new cover. Except that, by the time it is published, many of the phone numbers will already be out of date. Nevertheless, it seems that these books continue to sell very well.

There also appears to be a flourishing little industry publishing books about the Internet that are really picture books with long captions. These coffee-table pieces are mostly focused on producing very nice color reproductions of other people's Web pages. They are also filled with long explanations, just in case you won't get it when you view the Web site for yourself, or so it would seem. Often, these books take a full page or two to explain to readers what the subject Web site is all about and what its content really means. This is a very curious approach, since Web pages themselves are supposed to be designed to communicate their own message.

These types of books also tend to pontificate at length about how the Internet is a wonderful thing, giving us easy direct online access to these very Web pages. Agreed. But then why do they then proceed to circumvent our Internet experience with picture book explanations?. Maybe these books are a sales pitch promoting more use of the Internet. If so, they are pretty elaborate and expensive brochures.

Assuming that those books are selling, I can only conclude that this situation is an indication that there are obviously many people out there who are aware of and interested in the Internet, but who are not actually using it, for some reason. Rather, through these books they seem to be experiencing the Net vicariously. Either that, or Internet access is not available to them, and the books are the next best thing. I actually believe that the former premise is much more likely. In fact, I am convinced that many people still avoid getting connected to the Net due to their natural and understandable fear of "cyberspace" technology. After all, I know that it all sounded pretty scary to me at first.

This guide was written because I saw a practical need for it. I knew that my own journey of learning the basics of using the Internet by "the seat of my pants", stumbling blindly along, was not the ideal way for everyone to do it. Indeed if I could do it again, it would be different and less painful the next time around. Hindsight is a wonderful thing!

In particular, I remember how much all of the new technology intimidated me along the way. Not only was it hard to get a handle on it, even at the basic level, but it was constantly changing at a very rapid pace. In parallel with the Internet technology, all of the related computer hardware and software seemed also to be evolving on almost a monthly basis. This was a daunting scenario for anyone who happened to be a relative "non-tekkie" like me.

I also remember how every step of the way, in both books and in the everyday media, I was "shamed" into feeling totally inadequate just because I wasn't technically up-to-snuff with the "cyberworld." For example, the first few waves of Internet books were already describing people like me as "idiots" and/or "dummies". Right on their covers! Well maybe they had a point. But my question to them was and still is; "If you guys really think we are idiots and/or dummies, then why are you writing so-called 'beginners manuals' that are loaded with 'techno-babble', and weigh-in at over 300 pages in length?" Maybe *they* aren't quite as smart as they think they are, after all!

Consequently, this humble little guide is this author's attempt to put together a small manual (not much more than 100 pages was my target from the outset), that he wishes he had had when he first navigated the World Wide Web. Here's hoping that it helps you overcome any fears or misgivings you may have so that you too can take the plunge, get connected and have some fun!

About The First Revised Edition

The original version of this book was published in early 1999. Because things are changing so rapidly with respect to the Internet and the technological environment within which it operates I felt that an updated and expanded version was warranted to begin the new millennium. Accordingly, this first revised edition of the guide will be available in bookstores across North America sometime in the spring of 2000.

Minor revisions, updates and corrections have been made throughout the book. The most significant of these include: information on recent Internet developments, descriptions of new ways to access the Web, and the latest information on search engines and portals. A few more screen shot illustrations are included to help clarify certain points. Also, the number of Internet-related terminology definitions has been increased to more than 40, and the total researched sample Web sites has increased to 130. Finally, an entire new chapter titled "Nice To Know Information" has been added. It contains a compilation of helpful hints, useful facts and other value-added information that will prove very useful to the average Internet beginner.

to Leela
with love and gratitude

Part 1

Fear and the Internet

1. Introduction

The idea for this guide had been in the back of my mind for some four years before I actually sat down to write it. At least the seed was planted back then. That began a prolonged gestation period in late 1994, when I suddenly found myself in a situation where I was being forced to get "Internet-friendly" in a real hurry if I wanted to be successful in my university program.

Early Internet Experiences

During a six-month period, I received my Internet-baptism by fire. As with most things in my life, I did it the hard way. I plunged in blindly, hoping for the best. At that time, the popular and media "hype" about the Internet was just beginning to gather steam. However, I worked in an environment in which people were more technically inclined and interested than average.

Consequently, I was subject to an extra dose of that early hype, as well as the peer pressure that went along with it. Basically, the message I was getting from some of my colleagues and friends at the time was; "If you don't get up-to-speed with the Internet then you're not with the program."

Meanwhile, the media was just beginning its still torrid love affair with the Internet. It was not unusual at that time to hear and read references and advice on a daily basis about how one should not get left behind or become roadkill on the "information high-way". It seemed that everyone was talking about sending e-mails and surfing the Net. Whatever it all meant was very fuzzy to me at the time, but according to all reports the "net" was the way of the future. And who wanted to be left out of the future? Not me.

The way they were describing it at the time, the Internet sounded to me like some kind of new-fangled entertainment technology that was a sort of cross-over between the postal system and the telephone network, with television pictures thrown in. It appeared very complicated and of dubious serious value. Another "flavor of the month" phenomenon perhaps, I thought. On one level, I hoped it would all go the way of the 8-track cassette tape player in the 1970's, or Beta VCR's in the 1980's. As we all know by now, that definitely didn't happen.

Fear and Anxiety on the Internet

My first experiences with the Internet were not pleasant ones. At that time, most Internet users in my circle were hooked-up to public networks known as "Freenets". These networks may have been pioneering in many ways, but for the average user at the time, they were extremely tedious and frustrating, sporting technology that, by today's standards, was bordering on neanderthal. And contrary to current industry marketing hype, even today's technology still has a long way to go before being totally transparent, seamless, and intuitive to the average person.

For me, a typical Internet evening at the time involved many long and frustrating hours of fumbling around in "cyber-blackness". In fact, it frequently took an entire evening just to check my e-mail! More often than not, a session was prefaced by hours of busy signals before finally making a connection.

At that time, everything was text-based and menu-driven. Typically, the entire purpose of one of my sessions would be just to send and read a few e-mails. For a few of the more savvy "tekkie-types", it meant spending endless hours exchanging cyber-musings with like-minded "propeller-heads". These types were by far the most predominant Internet users at the time.

Even a very few years ago the Internet was certainly not anything close to a user-friendly communications tool, accessible to the average person. I would venture to say that, by today's still far from perfect standards, what they dubbed at the time as "surfing" the net could have been more aptly described as "stumbling around in the dark".

There Had to Be a Better Way

Many times, while tearing my hair out during those late night sessions, it occurred to me that if the Internet was going to be as universal as the pundits were predicting, there would have to be a better way to use it than there was available at the time. This wasn't difficult to perceive, since by then, most personal computer users were becoming familiar with the more user-friendly point and click interfaces of Macintosh and Windows. Meanwhile back on the Internet in 1994, most of us were still "hunting and pecking" our way around in cyber-darkness using our keyboards.

At the same time, just about every day in the newspaper, articles were appearing all about the totally "wired society" and how everyone was going to be plugged into the Internet in just a few short years. Knowing what I knew as a relatively early Internet user, I could never quite swallow those predictions at the time.

After all I reasoned, I was somewhat technically inclined and even I was finding the Internet access tools of the day to be awkward and counter-intuitive. I felt that the technology was forcing me to have to stumble and bumble around just to perform basic tasks, even though I was using what was then called "state-of-the-art" integrated technology.

Each time that I would make some sort of a "eureka" breakthrough on the Net using my trial-and-error learning process, I would think to myself; "If it is so difficult and frustrating for me, what about the poor people with little or no technical background or inclination?" I also wondered, "How can we even talk about the Internet being the way of the future for a wired society, when it is still a major technical production just to send and receive an e-mail?"

2. Background to This Guide

In Search of a Basic Guide

The need for a new kind of very basic guidebook like this one really started to crystalize in my mind in a serious way a couple of years ago. It was at that time that I decided to try and build my own Internet Web page. After all I reasoned, I had been a computer programmer at one time. Surely I could learn to build a basic Web page. I was also aware that even kids were doing it, so why not me?

Actually, the main reason why I decided to build a Web site on my own at that time was because I needed one for my new business. Yet, I felt that I didn't want to spend the $1,000 to $1,500 that people were telling me a new business-class Web site was going to cost. Also, I thought that I wouldn't be able to talk intelligently to the people who build Web sites unless I had some idea myself as to what was actually involved. In short, I didn't do it for fun, I did it because I felt I had no choice.

It was through this Web page building experience that I came to clearly realize that there is still a need out there for very fundamental instruction books or guides, for the average person who has no technical background or inclination at all.

Being "Non-Tekkies" Does Not Make Us "Dummies"!

In order to build my Web page I went out and bought one of those popular for "Dummies" books that I had seen lining the bookshelves of computer stores. This one was called "Creating Web Pages For Dummies". It was a hefty volume. Not only was it 357 pages long, but it was chock-full of technical terminology!

In the end, that book did turn out to be quite useful to me. Using it, combined with various other sources of basic information, I was able to create my own Web site over a two-week period. However, the first version of my relatively simple Web site probably took me between 60 and 80 hours of fumbling through the book, followed by trial and error scratching of my head, punctuated by desperate forays into other reference materials for additional clues. In other words, it was possible to do, but it definitely wasn't all that easy.

Fortunately, the "Dummies" book was quite well-written and well-organized, so I was able to follow it with a bit of effort. However, frequently during the process I wondered to myself one more time, "How on earth would the ordinary person with no computer-related technical background or inclination have any hope of doing what I was doing, even using such a book?" In other words, how could they possibly call this a beginners book?

I certainly didn't think that I was a "dummy" as was insinuated by me having to use that book in the first place. But on the other hand, maybe I was really dumb because I found their 357 pages of instructions just a little too technical for my liking. Interestingly, I recently checked-out one of the current best-selling "beginners" books for the Internet. It weighed in at a full 358 pages and is just jam-packed with technical jargon! In my opinion, this is a pretty heavy-handed approach for something supposedly aimed at neophytes.

The Problem With Most Internet "Guides"

Over the years I have frequently spent time leafing through some of the literally thousands of computer manuals that seem to proliferate out there in the marketplace. As mentioned earlier, I have even bought a number of them. However, with a few possible exceptions, usually by the time I get half-way through the Table of Contents of most of these books, my eyes tend to glaze over as my mind recoils with resistance due to all the "techno-jargon" I find there.

After all, I didn't want a degree in computer science! I just wanted to very quickly learn the most straightforward way to perform the basics of doing simple practical tasks so that my computer time could be productive personal time. I simply wanted to know how to "point and click" my way through with no muss, no fuss, and no unnecessary technical terminology.

Accordingly, the following are what I have perceived to be the major problems with most of the so-called "beginner" Internet guides that I have seen to date:

♦ They are usually written by "tekkies" for other tekkies. Even when they are trying not to, tekkies tend to get caught up in "teckno-speak" and appear to enjoy term-dropping, apparently it seems, to remind us of their intellectual superiority.

♦ They often patronize and talk down to "non-tekkies" just to make sure there will be no doubt as to the importance and in-dispensability of the tekkie authors and their colleagues.

♦ They average about 250 pages or more, and are filled with all kinds of unnecessary "static" and "white noise" in the form of jargon and teckno-speak that confuses and alienates ordinary people.

♦ They tend to insult the intelligence of most regular people by often giving detailed and lengthy descriptions of the contents of Web pages that most people are able to figure out for themselves once they get to that page. They don't seem to realize that for most of us, the challenge is the "getting there" part.

♦ They are usually written by so-called gurus and experts (often self-appointed), who seem to like to impress their friends and colleagues with their vast technical knowledge of the intricacies of the Internet as if they personally invented it.

♦ In between the techno-speak and the cyber-babble, many of these books make feeble attempts at "cutesy" down-home humor, which often has the effect of completely alienating the ordinary person who just wants the basic facts on how to get up-and-running on the Internet without the dumb (and often condescending) banter.

3. A Guide for the Ordinary Person

After my Web page building experience, I seriously started thinking about the problem of how one could relatively painlessly become "Internet-friendly" if one happens to be a non-tekkie, like most of us are. At first I assumed that there must be a proliferation of very basic beginner books out there for the true non-tekkies.

Nevertheless, I started to do a little bit of research and was somewhat surprised by what I found. It appeared that a basic step-by-step guide to getting started on using the Internet for total non-tekkies, of under 150 pages or so, did not seem to exist. Based on my recent research, this still appears to be the case. Maybe there is one out there somewhere, but I haven't found it yet.

Why This Guide Is Needed

Such a basic guide to the Internet is needed for a number of reasons:

♦ To take the fear and mystery out of the Internet, for ordinary people.

♦ To open up the Internet to tens of thousands of people who are avoiding it due to the fear and/or alienation associated with their negative perceptions of the technology involved.

♦ To provide a simple step-by-step guide that can be used by just about anybody to get connected to the Internet, and learn to use its basic functions.

♦ Because a very basic and simple guide to the Internet for the average person is long overdue.

Who This Guide Is For

♦ It is for the 70% or so of people in North America who have not yet used the Internet, or who have may have only sampled it in passing.

♦ It is for the other 10% to 15% of the people in North America who use the Internet but are not defined as regular users and may still have some basics to learn. That is, they do not fit the profile of regular users. These are defined as people who sign onto the Internet at least twice a week and also spend a minimum of two hours doing various things on the Net.

♦ In terms of types of people, it is for "technophobes" from all walks of life: seniors, homemakers, younger women and men, students and kids. Basically, regular people who already "have a life", and would like to keep one, while at the same time also becoming Internet-friendly. Typically, these individuals have well-balanced lives and do not want to spend endless hours glued to a computer monitor connected to the black hole of cyberspace. However, they do want to learn the basic functions of the Internet and to find out how it can be used as a tool to improve the quality and productivity of their daily lives.

Who This Guide Is Not For

♦ It is not for those ordinary people who are already knowledgeable, experienced, and reasonably adept Internet users; although they would probably find it to be a useful reference.

♦ It is definitely not for the more extreme Internet users who spend a good part of their lives connected to cyberspace. These people are also affectionately known by a number of terms including: tekkies, propeller-heads, cyber-surfers, geeks, cyber-heads, web-waifs, among others similar descriptors. By definition, this guide would not be needed by any of those people.

What This Guide Will Tell You

The whole point of this guide is to provide the reader with only the absolutely essential basics that one needs to know to become a functioning Internet user, capable of performing the main tasks that most people are interested in performing on the Net. Primarily those tasks are, how to surf the net, and how to send and receive e-mail. The operative term here is "need to know." This guide makes every effort to minimize extraneous static and unnecessary white-noise; namely, it deliberately omits the many facts and terms that are not absolutely required by a basic user.

What This Guide Will Not Tell You

This guide will definitely not tell you everything that there is to know about using the Internet. It is not intended to completely replace those 350-plus page volumes that are available on the subject of the Internet. Rather, this guide is designed to tell you only what you absolutely need to know to become functional on the Net. This is why the use of technical terms, cyber-babble and teckno-talk has been minimized.

For the reader's convenience, a short glossary of common Internet-related terms has been included in Chapter 9 for easy reference. Some of the terms defined there do not even appear in this book but, have been listed there since it is likely that readers will encounter them at some point in their early Internet explorations. With them defined here, one will at least understand some of the often extraneous, cyber-text that one will encounter at many Web sites and in some e-mails.

There Are Many More Complicated Books

There is a proliferation of more advanced manuals and handbooks out there in the marketplace that you may choose to pick up once you have learned the basics and decided that you would like to go further. As a word of caution, these books range from the intermediate level, up to very advanced. So be careful that you pick the next highest level of difficulty so that you can progress incrementally, one step at a time.

Terminology Used in This Guide

This guide is not for technical purists. Wherever possible it distills things down to their simplest levels, since that is its whole purpose. The terms Internet and Net are used interchangeably throughout this document. The terms World Wide Web (www) and Internet are also used interchangeably, although technically speaking, the Web is a sub-component of the Internet as a whole.

To assist the reader, capital letters are used throughout this guide to emphasize certain specific terms when they represent the proper technical name of a button, function or software program. For example, the term "Edit" would be capitalized to refer directly to the Edit function and/or button on the toolbar of a software program being discussed. In addition, some proper Internet technical terms are also capitalized for emphasis and to avoid confusion. Examples of these capitalized terms include: Internet (or Net), World Wide Web (or Web), Web page (or Page), Web site (or Site), Search Engine, Browser, Option, Edit, Back, Forward, Stop, Reload, Home, etc.

Again, every effort has been made to minimize the use of tekkie-terms unless absolutely necessary. As mentioned in the previous section, to help readers with the terminology of the Net, a glossary of short definitions of common Internet-related terms has been included in Chapter 9 for easy reference purposes.

Part 2

Overcoming the Fear

4. The Internet - A Brief Background

Put very simply, the Internet is a series of thousands of interconnected computer networks with a single point of access that connect the user to an electronic information system that spans the entire globe.

Although the Internet is made up of a number of sub-components, it is most widely known for its World Wide Web. The Web and E-mail are by far the most widely-used components of the Internet today.

Unlikely Beginnings

The seed of today's Internet was planted by the U.S. Department of Defense back in 1969 which established it as a network for communicating with its contractors around the world. By the mid-1980's the Internet was widely-used by the international scientific and academic communities to maintain contact and share information worldwide.

In those early days, the Internet was totally text-based and very rudimentary in function. It was not very user-friendly at all, and one had to be a bit of a "tekkie" to be able to use it effectively, which was fine for the predominantly technical users in those days.

The World Wide Web

Then in the 1990's, everything changed with the advent of the World Wide Web component of the Internet. With that breakthrough, came the implementation of graphics-based Browser software programs that created the first truly user-friendly interface between the Net and its users. Now as we begin the new millennium, the technology has developed to the point where the World Wide Web is an eclectic mingling of text, graphics, sound, and animated images.

The World Is Getting Wired

Estimates vary widely, but it is believed that the total number of people worldwide with Internet access in 1999 was somewhere in the order of 150 million to 175 million. Forecasters project that this number will grow to over 250 million by the year 2005. However, it should be noted that these figures do not necessarily represent regular or "active" Internet users. Putting it in terms of regular users only, the numbers would be more in the order of 125 to 150 million in 1999, and perhaps 225 to 250 million by the year 2005. Billions of e-mails are sent every day, adding up to trillions per year. These are huge numbers by any standard.

The Internet can now be accessed by people in almost 200 countries around the world, 24-hours a day, 365 days of the year. All one typically needs for personal access to the Net is a telephone line, a modem, and a personal computer with the appropriate computer software programs. In fact, for simple Internet access a computer is no longer mandatory due to the recent introduction into the marketplace of a number of "Internet appliances", as they are being called. Some of these devices are hand-held and some are wireless with no direct telephone connection required. "WebTV" is an example of this new class of Internet appliance. (see page 48). One can even access their e-mail on some cellular phones now. However, as pointed out earlier, similar to satellite communications and telephone systems, one does not need to know anything about how the Internet technology actually works to be able to use it effectively.

Many experts believe that the advent of the Internet is the most significant single technological event since the invention of the telephone, and that it will ultimately have more impact on human society than the Industrial Revolution has had.

5. Facing the Internet Head-On

When it comes to computer technology, fear of the unknown has always been a big one for me. Thus, when I started my first trial-and-error plunges into the Internet a few years ago, fear was definitely the operative word. This was especially the case before I started using the relatively user-friendly Browser programs that we have today.

Even though I knew that my fear was invariably irrational, I would often sit in front of the computer screen for long stretches of time, totally immobilized by a fear of pushing the wrong key and somehow destroying my computer or completely wrecking my hard-drive. Sometimes the block would be so great, I would lose interest in what I was doing and have to shut down the computer and walk away. I was even very reluctant to go to Web sites for fear of contracting some sort of computer virus, which the media was reporting at the time were lurking everywhere on the Net.

The Internet as the Unknown

In addition, the fact that I was connected to a worldwide network with many millions of other people who were also directly connected to the same network was very disconcerting to me. I often had the nagging feeling in the back of my mind that someone was watching my every keystroke and that once I made a false move, the Internet-police would be unleashed and reprimand me by e-mail! Who knows, maybe they would even cancel my access account if I screwed up badly enough! Not only that, but they and others would know that I was some kind of idiot for performing such a dumb move! Shame, shame.

Probably most of us can identify to some extent with this fear of technology phenomenon. Remember the early days of the automatic bank machines? How traumatic they were for some of us. I can still recall those first few hurried and uncertain online banking sessions, with a restless crowd breathing down my neck as I stood in front of the good old bank machine! How many of us have not experienced VCR-phobia at one point in our lives? It happened to me again just the other day. I still can't program the damn thing properly! To add insult to injury, they are now producing programmable televisions. I bought one a few months ago and am still referring to the user manual on a regular basis as I try to get all the functions to work properly.

You can imagine what it must have been like at the beginning of my career many years ago, as a computer programmer. The fear of somehow destroying a million dollar mainframe computer, or of a program going into a costly "infinite loop" were sometimes paralyzing. I would think it all over for hours sometimes before submitting my programs to the computer. Then I would finally hand it in, sweaty palms and all. One problem with that approach was that sometimes the sweaty palms would cause the punched cards of the day, to swell and bend and they would then jam in the card reader. A sort of self-fulfilling prophecy.

Fear of Technology is "Normal"

Suffice it to say that fear of the unknown is a basic part of the human condition for most of us. And for most of us, technology is a big unknown that we would rather not deal with most of the time. Thus, the fact that a good number of us suffer initially from varying degrees of "fear of the Internet" is not surprising. After all, it is a whole new frontier for many of us. And at first glance, the technology appears to be more complex than anything that we have ever been exposed to before. Here are some of the typical fears that I and many others have felt with respect to using the Internet.

♦ Maybe this is too complicated for me. Perhaps I won't be able to do it because I'm not a propeller-head or a computer-nerd.

♦ I have the feeling that if I do the wrong thing, or hit the wrong key I am somehow going to get sucked into the black hole of cyber-space.

- If I hit the wrong key or go to the wrong Web site, I might some-how damage my computer.

- If I go onto somebody's Web site I will unknowingly incur un-wanted financial charges.

- If I go onto somebody's Web site I will be exposing my computer to receiving an unwanted virus.

- I will be jeopardizing my personal security and privacy once I start "surfing" the Internet.

- Maybe "they" will cancel my account or send me a bill if I screw up badly enough!

Remember, these or similar fears are normal when faced with new technology like the Internet. As many psychologists would recom-mend, often the best way to defeat a fear is to face it head-on. Based on this author's personal experience with the Internet over the last few years, the psychologists are right on this point, espe-cially when it comes to de-mystifying something like the Net. You just have to practice "experiential learning" by diving into it head first, and soon the fear will disappear.

The Truth About the Internet

Accordingly, I strongly recommend that you live dangerously and just plunge straight into the Internet using this book as your guide. To ease any trepidation that you may have, as much as possible, try keeping the following "Internet truths" that I have discovered, in the forefront of your mind.

- **The Internet is just another new technology to be learned and mastered,** just like the latest telephone system, VCR, banking machine or personal organizer had to be mastered to improve your quality of life. In fact, learning to use the Internet is actually easier than it was to program many of the first gen-eration VCR's.

♦ **It's ok if you press the wrong key or click on the wrong Icon when surfing the Net.** You may not get the results you want, but you will not be damaging your computer or hard drive either. Don't be afraid to experiment by clicking on various Icons. No matter what happens, if you don't like the results you can immediately click on the Browser's "Back" button to escape.

♦ **Your computer being hooked-up to the Internet is not much more magical or mysterious than your television** receiving programs that you view by satellite, or making a direct long distance call to Nepal. It is just a sophisticated electronic communications tool, and you are the operator.

♦ **You are in control, and you are the master at all times,** whenever using your computer in conjunction with the Internet. You choose what to click and what not to click. You decide when to go forward and when to leave a Site.

♦ **You cannot be "sucked" into any place on the Internet where you don't want to go.** The content of the Internet is just like society at large. There are all types of people and sights to be seen, both good and bad (mostly good). Contrary to the media hype, people are not exposed to smut or hate on the Internet unless they choose to look for it. If one does just happen to stumble on to something unsavory by sheer accident, one can choose to not click on it and never return. It is always your choice.

♦ **People cannot read your e-mail until you send it to them.** Composing your e-mail is a totally private act. It only becomes public when you click on the "Send" button. Be careful about this one though, since sending e-mail is so easy and instantaneous. Often people click on the "Send" button in anger or haste and then immediately regret what they just sent. This author has learned the hard way, to always take a long pause before clicking on "Send". I usually stop and read, and sometimes re-read if necessary, any possibly sensitive e-mail. When you are reading it, think to yourself, "Would I want it to read like this if a copy was presented to me a month from now?" But make sure to practice prudence, not paranoia.

♦ **Your computer cannot contract a virus just because you have surfed the Net passively.** This can only happen if you choose to "download" a file from another Site or, if you choose to open an attachment to a suspicious e-mail from an unknown sender. Although overcoming the curiosity may be difficult sometimes, it is strongly recommended that you do not open any e-mail attachment that you are in any way unsure of. Remember, such decisions are always your choice – you are in control. When in doubt about a file to be downloaded or a suspicious e-mail, get an expert to check it out first, or simply delete it.

♦ **You cannot incur financial costs unless you first choose to** order something, and then also choose to provide a person or company with your credit card number or other billing information. Almost all Sites that allow you to purchase items online also allow you to choose to change your mind at the end of the ordering process, before the order is actually placed. Again, you are the one in control.

♦ **If in doubt back out!** If you ever find yourself somewhere you don't want to be on the Internet click on the "Back" button" of your Browser for immediate escape. A few disreputable sites actually disable the Back function when you are on their Site in an effort to try to force you to continue clicking forward at that Site. To escape in such cases, you can either type in a new Web Site url address in the Browser's site location line or you can click on the Home button.

♦ **No, there are no Internet police and nobody is watching your every move.** In fact, the Internet is one of the few true "anarchies" in which no person(s) or organization is in control. There is no Internet control or Internet headquarters. It's a loosely connected society with a set of "unofficial" protocols that have evolved from collective user experiences over the years. As one often reads in the paper, many sovereign-state governments don't like this aspect of the Net because they are preconditioned to want to control and regulate everything. However, the Internet is bigger than any one state or any group of nations. So far, the Internet has been doing a pretty fair job of democratic self-regulation.

♦ **Your privacy cannot be invaded via the Internet unless you allow it to be.** You decide who you give your e-mail address to. Unlike with telephones, there is no master directory of all e-mail addresses with which others can look you up. You give people permission to send you e-mails when you give them your e-mail address. So think carefully before you give it out. It's a hard thing to take back, and changing your e-mail address can be a real hassle. Nevertheless, protecting one's privacy on the Internet can be a little tricky these days. One must be very careful when registering at any Site on the Net, even recognized reputable sites.

Frequently, on the registration page you may find pre-checked button boxes giving the Site owner permission to use your e-mail address or other particulars to contact you in the future. Some may even pre-check a box saying that your information will be sold or given out to others. Consequently, be ever vigilant when registering at any Web Site and make sure that you disable any of these check boxes if you do not want unsolicited contact in the future. Most reputable Web Sites have a Privacy Policy available to consult on their Web Site. If in doubt, you can check this out before registering at a site. If there is no published privacy policy available you might want to think twice before registering at that particular site.

♦ **You do not have to be a technical genius to use the Internet.** As long as you can follow a few straightforward procedures that can be learned through simple repetition, you can be an active and productive Internet user. Remember, don't allow yourself to be intimidated by the technology or the tekkies. You are in charge. In fact, the reality is that you are as smart as, or even smarter than, many of the people who designed various technical components underlying the Internet. The technology is just another tool to be mastered.

Eventually, after lots of experience facing my fears of the Internet head-on, they mostly diminished into the background. In retrospect, I can see that these were an extreme version of similar fears I have felt facing other unknown technologies in my life. For example, the word "terror" would be more appropriate than "fear" in describing my state as a 17 year-old learning to drive a car equipped with a standard transmission and a clutch pedal!

The Internet Can Be Addictive

Yes, it is true that the Internet can become very addictive. It is available 24-hours a day, 7 days a week, 365 days a year, and gives a person access to more information and online activities than one could ever hope to experience in a lifetime. Spending countless hours on it can definitely be mood-altering, just like a powerful drug. I often found that after a few hours of "surfing", my mind would disappear into some sort of unconscious "dead zone" as I continued to point and click aimlessly.

This can happen to one very quickly. The ease of access and the 24-hour availability, coupled with virtually endless fascinating content can seduce one very easily. There is a never-ending series of literally hundreds of millions of hyperlinks that one could follow endlessly from site to site. Even today, if I'm not careful I can find myself arriving at a Web site after clicking on a series of hyperlinks, having completely forgotten what I actually set out to do 15 or 20 clicks before.

After experiencing some long overnight sessions when I was first connected to the Net I learned that I had to discipline myself, just to retain my sanity. Also, it was starting to cost me a small fortune in extra-hour connect charges. (Today, cost is no longer a barrier for most people as Internet access becomes cheaper). Now, I only go online on a "need to be there" basis. The moment I find myself clicking/surfing aimlessly from site to site without a real purpose any more, I know that I'm losing control, so I disconnect. Otherwise I could be there for days, lost in an endless black cyber-hole.

Part 3

Conquering the Internet

6. A Step-By-Step Approach to Using the Internet

The following steps have been formulated with the assumption that the reader is starting from close to absolute scratch as far as the Internet is concerned. The reader may or may not have a personal computer to begin with. This Chapter is organized into a logical and/or chronological sequence of eight Steps that move from the very beginning of the process, and then progress incrementally to the point where the reader will be relatively knowledgeable and familiar with the basic "need-to-know" functions of the Internet.

A note on the general terminology used in this guide was provided in Chapter 3, and some Common Internet Terms are defined in Chapter 9.

PCs versus Macintosh

For the convenience of those who may own Apple Macintosh computers, the equipment specifications pertaining to that specific brand of computer have been included in the Minimum Component List that follows. Otherwise, for the sake of simplicity, it has been assumed throughout the following Steps that an IBM compatible PC clone personal computer is the type of computer being used.

These PC computers account for about 90% of all personal computers in use in North America at this time. In any case, when it comes to using the Internet, after the initial stage of configuring (setting-up) the computer and related software is complete, it is normally irrelevant whether one is using a PC or a Macintosh.

Netscape Navigator vs. Microsoft Explorer

These are by far the two most popular graphics-based Internet Browser software programs. They act as the direct connection between the user and the Internet. They are almost identical in function, with a few minor technical and terminology differences. Netscape Navigator was the first major Browser program to proliferate the Internet. Microsoft Internet Explorer was developed after NS-Navigator, and is essentially its functional clone. Because of their equal popularity today, both of these Browser programs will be referenced during the explanation of the following Steps. When you get to the sections that pertain to the "other" Browser, you can just skip them.

Netscape's latest Internet Browser suite is called Netscape Communicator. This package consists of Netscape Messenger for e-mail, Netscape Composer to publish html Web pages, and Netscape Navigator as the actual Browser program. NS-Navigator is still considered to be the most widely used stand-alone Browser.

As with most competing software programs these days, when each company produces the latest version of its Browser, they try to make whatever small incremental improvements they can over the most recent version of the competitor's product. Then the competing company follows-suit when it next issues its latest version; and so goes the software development and marketing cycle.

However, the technology has reached the point where there is only so much that a company can do in refining Browser software. This author has copies of both NS-Navigator and MS-Explorer, and has used both. It just so happens that NS-Navigator was the first one I used, so I am a tad more comfortable with it. As is the case with most software programs, people tend to favor the first one they used because it is familiar to them. For most people, learning a new program just means more frustration and inconvenience during the learning process, so they generally don't like to switch from the one they already know.

In short, with my apologies to software sales people, as far as this author is concerned, when it comes to MS-Explorer versus NS-

Navigator it is essentially "six of one and half a dozen of the other."

STEP 1 – Getting the Minimum Required Equipment

The following figure displays the recommended minimum computer component requirements to effectively access and use the Internet via personal computer.

These are what this author considers to be the minimum basic hardware and software requirements if you were buying a new computer. If you already have a computer, it is suggested that you upgrade to these levels. To buy such a system from scratch will typically cost you somewhere between $1,000 and $1,500 once you have all the hardware and software. Although not absolutely necessary, you might want to add a CD-ROM drive when purchasing a new system, since most new software comes in CD-ROM format these days.

Figure 6-1: Minimum Component List

COMPONENT	STANDARD PC	APPLE PC
Operating System	Windows 95 or 98	Mac O/S 7.5
Memory	16 Mbytes RAM	16 Mbytes RAM
Power/Speed	486 or Pentium	68040 chip
Hard Disk Drive	200 Mbytes	200 Mbytes
Free Disk Space	35 Mbytes	30 Mbytes
VGA Graphics Card	256 Colors at 640 x 480 res.	256 Colors at 640 x 480 res.
Modem	28.8 baud	28.8 baud
Browser	NS-Navigator or MS-Explorer	NS-Navigator or MS-Explorer

Maybe You Don't Need A Computer

As mentioned in the previous chapter, with the rapid development of technology it is now possible to access the Internet without using a personal computer. New devices, generically known as "Internet appliances", are now being produced by a number of different manufacturers and the features vary from maker to maker. They range in price between $100 and $500. Standard ISP Internet access arrangements and charges usually apply. The development of such products has arisen out of the very real and legitimate need of many people for simple uncomplicated access to the Internet so that they can do basic things such as sending/receiving e-mails and simple Web browsing.

Although these new Internet appliances eliminate the need for a personal computer to perform the basics on the Web, the first generation of these devices does have some limitations and drawbacks. For example, they cannot handle either sending or receiving e-mail attachments. One still needs a PC to process these. Also, since they have very small screens compared with a PC they require special browsers that usually have character format restrictions to handle text and images for the small screens. Nevertheless, for some people these appliances may be the ideal solution. Example's of these new Internet appliances include: InfoGear's iPhone, Cidco's Mail Station, and Netpliance's iOpener.

An interesting compromise that has recently emerged is the move by some of the major personal computer manufacturers to produced stripped-down "Internet computers." These are basic PC's that offer the bare minimum of features that are required by individuals and small businesses to access and use the Internet. The package normally includes a small PC, a monitor and a printer, all with simple installation and operation features. These new iPC's start in price as low as $500 which makes them directly competitive with the Internet appliances price-wise; and they generally offer more features. Early examples of these include: Dell's Webpc, Compaq's iPaq and Advanced Micro Device's Easy-Now.

You Don't Need to Understand the Details

In fact, I'm sure you don't want to. You just have to believe that you do not have to know the technical meanings or intricacies of any of the items or terms listed on the foregoing Minimum Component List. You can simply take the list to your computer dealer and tell them that it is your minimum requirement, and that you want the best price possible for such a set-up. Also, tell them that you want them to set everything up for you as a condition of the sale. If they have a problem with that, you can always go elsewhere. These days, most computer stores have their own technicians who can set you up completely in as little as an hour. Then you just have to take the components home and plug them in as per the instructions they give you.

Your computer may still operate with the Internet if it has less capacity than some of those listed in the Minimum Component List. However, its performance will probably be marginal. For example, it is possible to browse the Net with slower speed modems of 9,600 baud or 14,400 baud, but the process will be excruciatingly slow. That is why a 28,800 baud modem is recommended as a minimum. If you can afford a faster one than that, by all means get one. In fact, these days, most new personal computers come with a standard pre-installed 56,000 baud modem.

Purists and tekkies could debate endlessly whether you need the minimum capacities listed in Figure 6-1, or whether you need a bit more, or if one could get by with a bit less. This component list is considered by this author to be the ideal minimum configuration to provide you with a rewarding and hassle-free Internet experience.

You Don't Need a Separate Telephone Line

Some people are under the impression that a special and/or separate telephone line is required to access the Internet. Neither is true. Any standard phone line works. However, one may choose to have a separate line installed if Internet usage gets too high, because it does prevent the line from being used for other purposes.

Most casual users tend to get by with just the one line, keeping their sessions short, or by doing their Internet work late at night or early in the morning. You will know whether you need to get a separate line after a few weeks of being connected, if it becomes a major issue around the house that you can't resolve by rescheduling your sessions.

With the new high-speed access service offered by some telephone companies it is now possible to talk on the telephone and access the Internet at the same time using the same phone line. This effectively eliminates the need for a second telephone line.

STEP 2 – Finding an Internet Service Provider

Also known as an ISP, an Internet Service Provider is a company that offers the basic connection services that you need in order to connect your computer to the Internet. It's sort of like a telephone company for the Internet. In fact, many telephone companies also act as ISP's. There are hundreds of ISP's in North America. Fundamentally, they all offer the same basic services. However, it is a very competitive business and they will go all out to get you as a customer by telling you that their product is better and somehow different from that of their competitors. This is usually sales and marketing hype. It is very similar to the head-to-head, and sometimes aggressive competition among telephone companies for long-distance customers.

Choosing an ISP

The easiest way to find an ISP in your area is to ask your friends and colleagues, or you can look in the yellow pages under Internet Services. ISP's often run advertisements in the local newspaper or the TV guide. When choosing an ISP, the main factor will be cost.

ISP's normally offer various packages based on the number of hours of connect-time required per month. For example, my ISP offers a basic package of 10 hours of total monthly connect time for $9.95. Additional hours cost $1.50 each. As long as you stay under the 10 hours it's a reasonable deal, but after that it starts to get pricey. The deal I have right now gives me 60 connect hours per month for $15.95. I have never exceeded this amount, as I usually come in at between 30 and 40 hours per month.

There are much better "deals" out there than the one that I have, but for me its worth a couple of extra dollars in expenses, to not have to change my e-mail address, as I would be forced to do if I moved to another ISP. In addition, I am receiving a relatively high level of service that I am satisfied with.

Most companies offer a range of packages depending on your expected level of usage. For example, after $9.95 for 10 hours per month, my ISP offers 20 hours of connect time for $12.95 per month with additional hours at $1.50 each. Some companies offer bulk flat-rate packages such as $29.95 per month for unlimited hours. It all depends on your needs.

I suggest you try what I did, and start with the basic package for a month or two, watching that you don't go too far over the limit and incur too many extra-hour charges. Then, after you get a feel for how you use the Internet on an ongoing basis, you can arrange for your ISP to move you to another level of package.

Just to give you a feel for it, I personally log onto the Internet three to four times a day, mostly to read and send e-mail and to send/receive electronic documents. In addition, I conduct online research on various subjects on a regular basis. As I stated above, at this kind of activity level, I usually manage to stay between 30 and 40 of connect-time in a typical month. On the other hand, I know that there are many Internet geeks and/or addicts who spend up to 100 hours per month online! You may know some of these people too.

Free Internet Access

A few companies are now offering free Internet access. However, as with most things that are free, there is a catch. In exchange for the free service, the user has to agree to be exposed to a steady diet of online advertisements which they then have to click on from time to time during their session in order to stay connected. This free access model, which is still experimental, assumes that the extra advertising revenues attributable to the new free service users will at least cover the cost of providing the service.

To-date no one is making money offering this free access, and experts are skeptical as to whether the average Internet user will ever agree to be bombarded by a constant stream of ads on a long-term basis. There are also concerns about whether such free service providers will provide quality content and ancillary services, both of which are expensive to maintain, or whether their focus will be strictly on raw access to the Internet. An example of this free Internet access service can be found at: **www.altavista.digital.com.**

High-Speed Internet Access

In many parts of North America, some Internet Service Providers are now offering high-speed Internet access. There are basically two types of high-speed access available; cable based and telephone based, and they are typically offered by cable television companies or telephone companies, respectively. The claims are that these services operate at anywhere from 15 to 100 times as fast as a 56K modem. These speeds are quite amazing but for the average user wanting to do some e-mailing and a bit of simple Web surfing, this is definitely overkill. A 56K modem on a middle of the road PC is plenty of speed for the average user.

A typical high-speed access user at this time, would be a company or individual that uploads and downloads multi-media presentations that include lots of video clips and sound tracks. Even then, 95% or more of the existing Web sites do not yet offer content that requires the use of a high-speed connection. There are also pros and cons related to both of the new high-speed technologies and it isn't clear which one will end up as the standard. Including the rental of a required special modem, high-speed access costs two to three times what a basic standard Internet service costs today.

Unless you have some compelling reason to do so, this author would discourage you from buying high-speed Internet access until it is a cost-effective alternative for the average user and the majority of Web sites offer high-speed features.

Look for Value-Added Services

When searching for an Internet Service Provider look for one that offers a set of value-added services as part of their package price. For example, some will offer a 1-800 technical support "hotline", 24-hours a day. Other ISP's will offer extensive "gateway" services through their welcoming home page that will give you instant access to a wealth of information services and resources at your fingertips, whenever you connect to your ISP's Web site.

This type of gateway service saves you the trouble of having to search the Web for all kinds of information. However, sometimes it can also result in information overload. My experience has shown that after you become confident and familiar with getting around the Net, you will have your own personally customized list of information services.

The Internet service provider that I have been with for a few years now also offers free space on its server (computer) for me to build and maintain a personal or business Web site. This comes for free as part of the standard package. With another ISP charging separately for this service, it would be a significant cost for me.

Remember, there is a lot of competition out there, so ask your Internet-friendly friends and colleagues who they think offers the best overall deal. One word of caution, if someone mentions frequent busy signals, I would suggest avoiding that ISP since it means that they have insufficient equipment and infrastructure to support their existing subscriber base. Ask around and shop around before you sign up.

When estimating your expected connect-time hours initially, remember that it is likely that your usage will be a little bit higher than expected at first. But, after the novelty wears off, your connect time will probably drop off somewhat. One also becomes more efficient using online connect-time with more experience. On the other hand, you may become an "Internet addict" and end up requiring one of the unlimited flat rate packages.

Commercial Online Services

There are a number of large companies that are known as "commercial online services companies". A couple of them have been around since the Internet became available to the general public in the mid-1990's. The primary online services are: America Online, Compuserve, Prodigy and The Microsoft Network. They offer a wide variety of services that are not offered by most standard ISP's. Essentially, they provide their users with a "one-stop-service portal" with which to access the World Wide Web.

The portal they offer is a friendly and comfortable environment for users, providing all kinds of pre-packaged consumer and information services, instantly available to subscribers with just a point and a click of the mouse. One can also access the Web directly from the online service portal to go out and find one's own services on the Net.

However, the online service companies usually charge a flat rate that is not necessarily the most cost-effective Internet access solution for many people. Many of the services that one pays for through a subscription to a commercial online service provider are actually available elsewhere on the Web for free, or at a much lower cost. Some of the major online services have also come under criticism from time to time for not being able to support their large user-bases with adequate computer and telecommunications equipment.

As the Internet matures, the differentiation in services offered by these online service companies and many of the large ISP's and search engine portals is diminishing, as the latter continue to improve their content and range of services. Nevertheless, some people may choose to pay a bit of a premium in dollars and level of service to have access to a protected pre-packaged environment that can be provided by a commercial online service provider.

STEP 3 – Getting Connected to the Internet

Once you have your minimum computer equipment components as per the previous step, the next thing to do is to get the required software loaded onto your computer so that you can access the Internet. Normally, this software will be supplied by your ISP in pre-packaged "ready-to-load" form, either on a diskette or a CD-ROM.

It Can Be Complicated

This phase can be a somewhat complicated process, or it can be very simple, depending on how you approach it. I could totally confuse and alienate you now by doing what most Internet books do; that is, provide you with two or three pages of detailed technical instructions on what might, or might not, happen when you attempt to load the software yourself. But inflicting that kind of pain on you is not what this guide is about. Besides, more often than not, I find that my particular situation or configuration is somehow slightly different than the hypothetical one covered in the manual. So I end up having problems anyway.

It Can Also Be Simple

Consequently, my strong recommendation is that you keep it as simple as possible by relying on your ISP to "hold your hand" through the process. Before you sign on with an ISP, plead absolute ignorance of computers and modems and ask them how they plan to set up your computer for the Internet. For those of you who want to take a stab at it yourselves, most ISP's will provide you with diskettes or CD-ROM's that should walk you through the connection set-up process relatively painlessly.

Figure 6-2 – Connecting to Your ISP

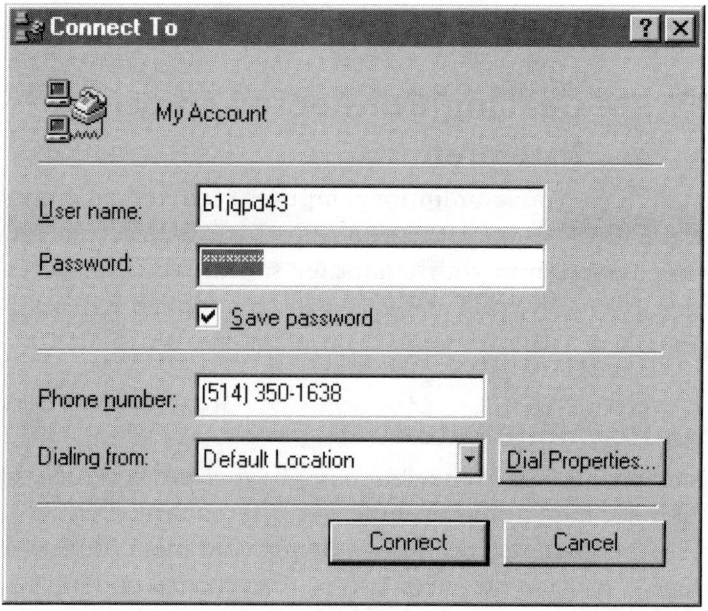

Watch Out for "Compatible" and "Integrated"

However, I will caution you here that the terms "total compatibility" and "completely integrated" are used very loosely by computer sales and marketing people. In my experience, it has been rare that I have loaded major new software onto my computer or connected new hardware, without a number of technical "glitches". This is especially the case when telecommunications equipment such as modems and telephone systems are involved, as is the case with an Internet connection.

Let Someone Else Do It for You

But remember; you don't have to do it yourself and don't feel pressured into doing so. After all, when was the last time you fixed your television or adjusted the fuel injection in your car? You are not doing this to become a computer geek. All you really want is to get your computer set-up so that you can access the Internet. There are many people who would be happy to do this for you. All you want in the end, is a little Icon on your computer screen that, when double-clicked by your mouse, will activate the modem to dial the telephone and connect your computer automatically to the Internet.

Your ISP Can Help

If you are nervous or unsure about this step, ask a computer-friendly friend or acquaintance who has already been through the process to help you. If that is not possible, you can always call the ISP's user-support hotline for help in setting up. Any decent ISP will have such a service.

So Can the Local Computer Store

A simple approach that I have used many times when installing new software and hardware that I was unsure of, is to take my computer to the nearest computer store. (i.e. just the box part; not the monitor, printer, etc.) There, technicians can install and test the software. Sometimes, they will do this free of charge, or they may charge you a small fee for their time. Typically, it will take from 15 to 30 minutes of their time to install and test Internet access software for you. The good thing about this approach is that after they finish the installation, they will usually be happy to walk you through a hands-on demonstration. A sort of impromptu free training session often results.

STEP 4 – Figuring Out Your Internet Browser

Once your computer is all ready to connect to the Internet, if the set-up is correct, all you will have to do is double click your mouse on one Icon. This will activate your modem and automatically dial-up the Internet via your ISP company's computer. During this process you will see a dialogue box similar to that shown in Figure 6.2. To proceed, double-click on the Connect button and then enter your password when prompted.

The first thing you will see when you are connected is an opening Web page. The opening page that you see, will vary depending on the Browser that you are using, and whether your ISP has pre-set its own Home page as your opening page. The opening page can be changed by you as one of the Options in your Browser.

Whatever your opening page is set to does not matter because it is just your starting point. The important thing when you see an opening page is that you are now connected to the Internet. From that "jumping-off page" you can go wherever you like on the World Wide Web simply by pointing and clicking your mouse.

NS-Navigator and MS-Explorer

As mentioned earlier, the two Internet Web Browsers that proliferate the Internet are Netscape Navigator and Microsoft Explorer. These Browser programs are simply the tools one uses to navigate around and perform tasks on the Internet. In terms of functionality, these two Browsers are virtually identical. The NS-Navigator and MS-Explorer opening windows are shown in Figure 6-4 and Figure 6-5, respectively. Figure 6-3 on the next page shows the important navigational function buttons/labels that you will see on the top-of-the-page toolbar in the window of whichever Browser you are using, (i.e. NS-Navigator or MS-Explorer) and briefly describes their function. Just a single click of your mouse on any one of them will activate your chosen function.

Figure 6-3 Browser Functions and Attributes

NS-Navigator Buttons	MS-Explorer Buttons	Function/Remarks
Netsite Line	Address Line	This is the white horizontal bar or space just below the toolbar where the current URL address appears. You can change this address by highlighting the area and then typing in whatever new address you wish.
Back	Back	This button retraces your previous steps during the current session. A gray-shaded button means there are no more backward steps.
Forward	Forward	This is to reverse your direction after you have used the Back button. It allows you to retrace your steps to where you were before you started going back.
Reload	Refresh	This will give you a new version of the Web page that you are currently looking at. Use this whenever the downloaded page in your window appears to be incomplete, garbled, or distorted. This just happens sometimes.
Stop	Stop	This is your "escape" button. Click on it, and it will stop the current task and allow you to do something else. Note: Don't worry, it will not terminate your session!
Home	Home	Takes you back to your pre-defined original starting page.
Print	Print	This will print the current Web page you are viewing in your Browser.
Bookmarks	Favorites	These allow you to save or mark the information about wherever you are on the Net so that next time you can go there directly. (see Step 7).
Status area	Status area	A blank area in the lower left-hand corner of the window that displays such things as the status of the download of the current page and where you will go if you click the next link. For information purposes only.

These are the "need-to-know" buttons for navigating the Web with your Browser program. Both NS-Navigator and MS-Explorer have a number of other functions as well, but they are not essential to normal operations (eg. Search, Shop, etc). To review these other functions, you can do some point and click experimentation as you see fit.

Figure 6-4 – Netscape Navigator Opening Screen

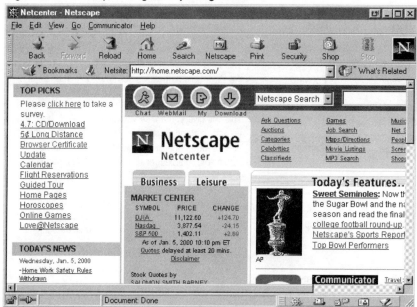

On the upper right-hand corner of both NS-Navigator and MS-Explorer you will see a small logo for the respective Browser. When images and data are being downloaded behind the scenes in response to one of your mouse clicks, small streaks of light or other types of movement will appear in the logo window. This is normal, and for information/status purposes only. It is simply an indication that the Browser is still busy doing what you asked it to do. Normally, when the requested pages have been completely downloaded into your Browser, the movement stops. Clicking on the Browser Logo will take you to the Home Page of the Browser manufacturer.

Figure 6-5 – Microsoft Internet Explorer Opening Screen

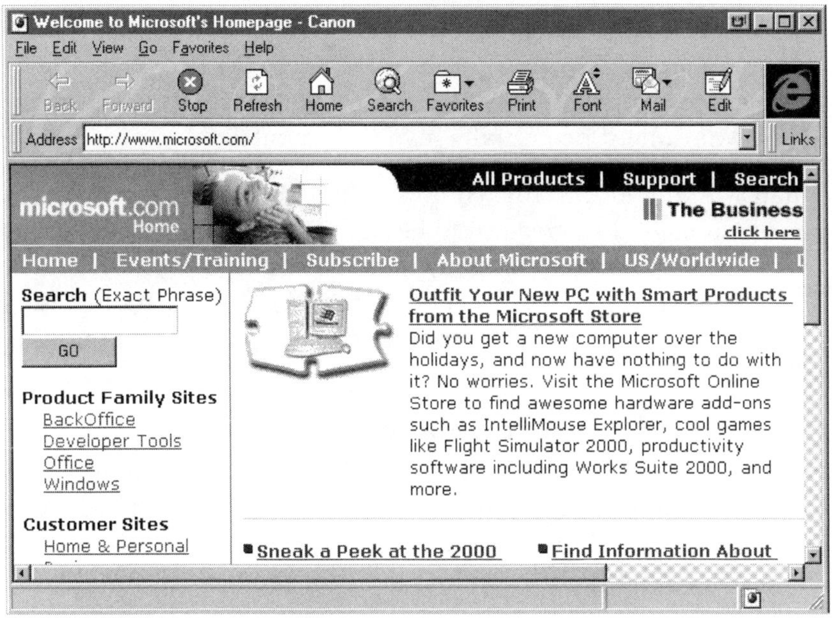

Don't Be Afraid To Experiment

I suggest you spend some time experimenting in your first session or two. Go ahead and click on anything that you are curious about. If a function button does something you don't want it to, you can always reverse the operation by choosing the previous setting. If you click on something and it takes you to another Page and you don't want to be there, you can simply click on the Back button to return to your original spot. If you ever click on something and your Browser seems like it has gotten lost in cyberspace, click on either Stop or Reload/Refresh.

STEP 5 – Surfing the Net with Your Browser

Surfing the Net is just Internet slang for moving or linking from Web site to Web site on the World Wide Web. It is simply that, and nothing more. I remember a few years ago when I first heard and read about people "surfing" the Net, it sounded both mysterious and complicated. This is another case where the "in" term among the tekkies conjured up all kinds of unnecessary fears in me about what might be actually involved in "surfing".

When I finally found out what "surfing" the Net really meant, I almost choked! It turned out to be nothing more than being in my Browser program and using my mouse to point and click my way around the Internet whenever I would see a little hand that I wanted to click on! This was not so technically challenging after all!

Clicking On the Little Hand

As you move the mouse pointer around the current Web page that you are viewing, you will notice that, from time to time, as you pass over a graphical object or an underlined word, a little hand will appear. This little hand means that there is an underlying "link", and if you click on that spot where the hand is, you will be taken to another Web page on the same Web site or, to an entirely different Web site. These are known as links. Links in text are always underlined and usually, but not always, they are colored blue. Invariably, they will sprout a little hand. Links are what move you around from place to place on the World Wide Web. Graphical pictures that sprout little hands as your mouse pointer passes over them are also links.

Entering A Web Address Directly

If you already have a Web site address that you want to check out when you connect to the Net, you can simply type it straight into the Netsite/Location Line (NS-Navigator), or Address Line (MS-

Explorer) of your Browser. This can be slightly tricky. First you have to use the mouse to highlight in blue the text of the address that is already in that Line. Then, you click the cursor in the exact position in the line where you want to begin entering the new address. The blue highlighting should disappear at this point and the cursor will be pulsating in the position you have placed it in. At that point you type in the entire new address making sure you delete any characters remaining from the old address on the right-hand end. Then, press the Enter/Return key and you will be taken directly to the new address.

For practice, try clicking on as many links as you like, just to see where they take you. Remember you always have the Back, Forward and Stop buttons to either retrace or terminate your steps.

Ending Your Internet Session

You can end your Internet session at any time you like. You do this by exiting your Browser program first. This is done by clicking on the X in the upper right-hand corner of the Browser window. This will terminate your session and disconnect you automatically from your ISP service. As you exit, you may receive some messages asking you to confirm what you want to do. Just go ahead and answer yes or no as the situation and your preferences dictate.

STEP 6 – Using a Search Engine to Find Things

Once you start to search the Web for information of specific interest to you is when you will truly begin to comprehend the power of the Internet. With just a few clicks of the mouse you can search databases stored on tens of thousands of computers all over the world. In another few clicks you can travel electronically all over the globe. Personal experience has shown me that doing research on the World Wide Web can be both exciting and rewarding due to its sheer power in terms of depth, breadth, and immediacy.

There Is No Central Internet Directory

Getting connected to the Internet is one thing. Knowing where you want to go is a whole other issue. As explained earlier on, the Internet consists of millions of computers linking many millions of people. It also consists of millions of Web sites with millions of Web pages, containing billions of pieces of information, any one of which you may be interested in. However, there is no comprehensive central Internet telephone-type directory that lists all possible sites. And because of the decentralized nature of the Internet, there will never be one such authoritative source of all information. This is why Search Engines were invented.

A Search Engine Is an Index

Search Engines are powerful computer programs that are constantly scanning the World Wide Web and adding new information about Web pages and Web sites that they find, and then updating their own internal indexes. You can then use one or more of these Search Engine Indexes to find Sites and Pages relating to your own topics of interest. In theory, Search Engines allow one to search the entire contents of the World Wide Web, based on how it existed at one specific point in time. Most of these indexes are being updated on a daily basis, so it is possible that new information for the same search criteria may appear from one day to the next.

Studies conducted in 1999 found that there are somewhere between 800 million and 1 billion pages of text on the Internet with thousands of pages being added each day. The surveys revealed that even the major search engines cannot keep up with all of the content that is being generated. In fact, it was found that the search engines with the widest coverage are listing only between 16% to 18% of the total pages available on the Web. The Search Engine with the most extensive index lists between 140 million and 160 million pages.

A Sample Search

To use a Search Engine, just go to its Web address by typing its URL into your Browser Location or Address line, followed by Enter. When you link to the Search Engine page, you will be asked to enter a word or phrase that best describes what you are searching for. For example, if you were interested in finding information about botanical gardens you would naturally enter the

Figure 6-6 – NS-Navigator Search Results Using Alta Vista

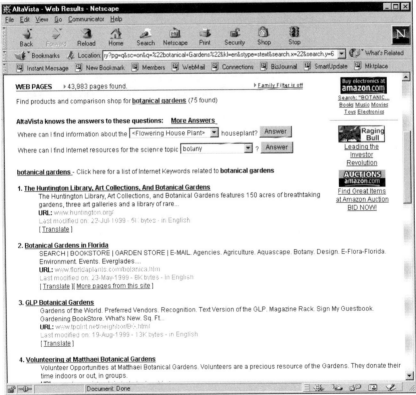

term "botanical gardens". Normally, within two or three seconds you will be presented with a message that tells you how many occurrences of your "botanical gardens" phrase was found. What the particular Search Engine considers to be the best matches will be listed first. Each listing will contain a live URL address link that you may click on so that you can go directly to that Site or Page from the Search Engine.

Narrowing Down a Search

When you do an initial search, don't panic if you are informed that some huge number of occurrences such as 200,000 or more, were found! You will notice that after reviewing the first 20 or so "hits" as they are called, the references to what you are specifically looking for become more and more indirect and obscure.

Figure 6-7 – MS-Internet Explorer Search Results Using Yahoo!

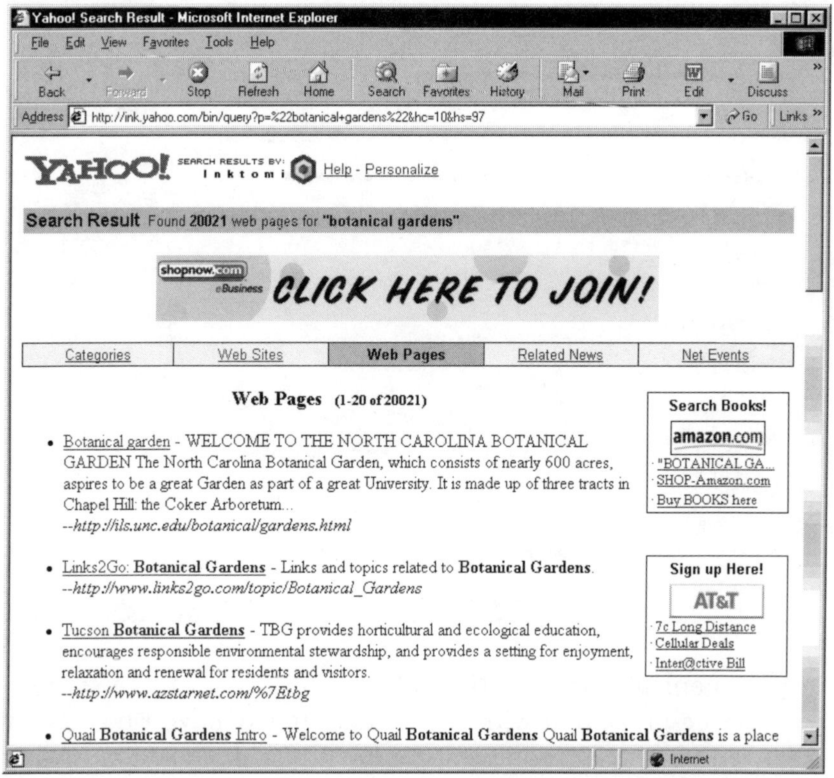

This is because they always list the "best results" first. In some cases, you may want to narrow a search down a little more specifically. To do this, some Search Engines allow you to enter "Boolean strings." This is simply a search technique based on a certain type of mathematical logic called "Boolean algebra" which is named after the inventor-mathematician George Boole. Most Search Engines also have other options for "refining" searches and carry detailed explanations on how to use these.

Using the botanical gardens search from the previous example, an "open" (i.e. non-Boolean) type of search would list all Web sites and Web pages that contain the word "botanical" or the word "gardens". On the other hand, a Boolean search would allow you to request a listing of only those sites and pages where both "botanical" AND "gardens" occur. For compound, and more complex searches, this capability can be very helpful in narrowing down a search. The search "refine" options of some of the Search Engines work very effectively as well.

Major Search Engines

There are over 1,500 Search Engines and indexes on the World Wide Web. However, there are about a dozen or so major ones. It is estimated that the following 12 Search Engines collectively cover between 40% and 50% of all of the pages on the World Wide Web.

AllTheWeb	**at**	www.alltheweb.com
Alta Vista	**at**	www.altavista.digital.com
Euroseek	**at**	www.euroseek.net
Excite	**at**	www.excite.com
Google	**at**	www.google.com
HotBot	**at**	www.hotbot.com
Infoseek	**at**	www.infoseek.com
Lycos	**at**	www.lycos.com
Microsoft	**at**	www.msn.com
Northern Light	**at**	www.northernlight.com

Snap   **at** www.snap.com
Yahoo!   **at** www.yahoo.com

Most people tend to favor one or two of these as their Search Engines of choice. For example, I always start my searches with Alta Vista since it is reputedly the one with the most Web pages listed. (they claim over 140 million page listings). Also, I like the look and feel of Alta Vista, and the way that it displays search results. In cases where I can't find exactly what I am looking for, or when I want more choices, I then move to Yahoo! or Excite to do some more searching. As stated earlier, the Search Engines you choose are a matter of personal choice. Use the ones that you feel most comfortable with, and which seem to return the best results for your type of searching.

Search Results Will Vary

When working with Search Engines, it is important to know that each one, given exactly the same search criteria keyword will return somewhat different results.(see Figures 6-6 and 6-7.) This is because each one of them uses its own secret/proprietary search formula, and each one also relies upon many different sources of Web site and Web page registration information. Because of this, it is a good idea to try two or three Search Engines if you want to be fairly certain that you are seeing pretty well everything that is out there on the Web which matches your criteria.

And remember, just because you find some information out there on the World Wide Web does not necessarily mean that it is correct. Anyone can put up a Web page or create a Web site. So there is also a lot of garbage out in the Wide World Web, meaning that you will have to be discriminating in your searches.

The Power of Meta Search Engines

The existence of Meta Search Engines is one of the most exciting discoveries I have made on the Internet in the past year. Meta simply means that these are Search Engines of a higher, or second, order. These are very powerful Search Engines designed to save you time and increase your productivity at the same time. What Meta Search Engines do for you is, for a particular search term, they search the results of a number of the major regular Search Engines and return an aggregate search result to you. In other words, they eliminate the need for one to have to conduct searches for a particular term in each one of the major conventional search engines! There are about 100 Meta Search Engines available right now but to-date I have only found the need to try a few of them. My favorite one so far can be found at **www.mamma.com.**

Figure 6-8 – Search Results Using Meta Search Engine Mamma.Com

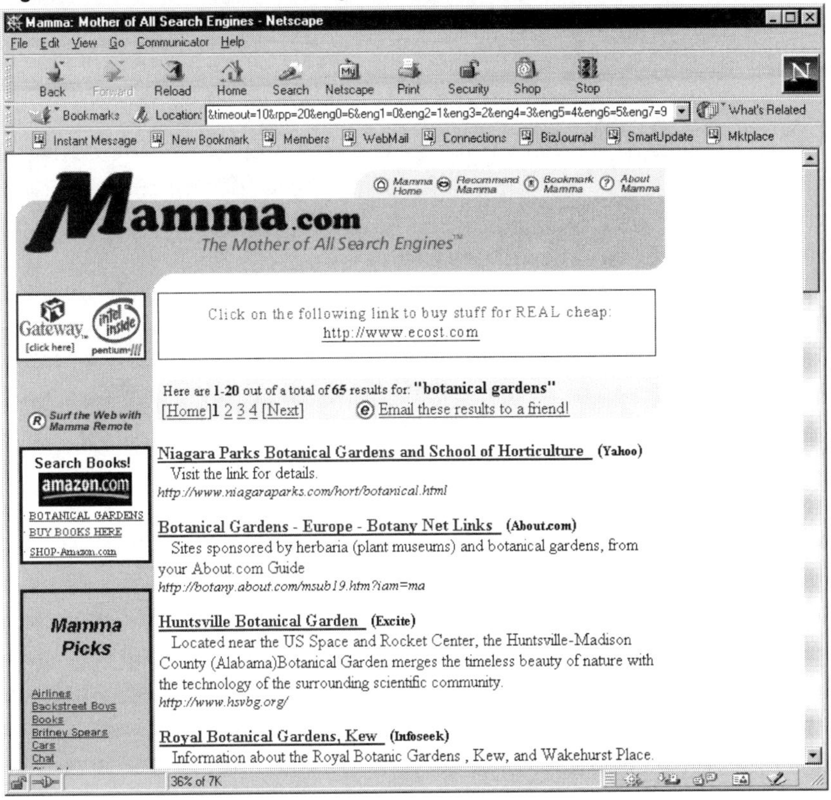

Figure 6-8 is an example of a search conducted using the Meta Search Engine www.mamma.com. When one enters a search term into mamma.com, that service instantly re-submits the search term to eight the top conventional Search Engines on the Internet. It then captures the results returned from those individual searches, eliminates duplicates, redundancies and poor matches, and then displays the mamma.com integrated and consolidated search results. For each listing returned it also displays under which of the conventional engines the listing was found. As a result the user gets much cleaner and more relevant search results. Typically, mamma.com will list something like 48 results for an entire search, and all of them will be excellent matches. This is compared with the thousands of results that will be returned by the typical standard search engines, full of duplicates, redundancies and poor matches.

For someone conducting a lot of online research, these Meta Search Engines are definitely an improvement over the conventional models due to the savings in time and productivity that they offer. An extensive list of Meta Search Engines can be found at: **www.metasearchengines.com.**

Some Tips For Web Searching

Learning how to search for information on the Internet using Search Engines is more a matter of practice than anything else. I suggest you start doing some practice searches in your first few Internet sessions. Pretty soon you will have worked out your own personal search techniques that work best for you. The following are a few things that I have learned about searching for information while using Search Engines:

♦ **Bookmark a Favorite "hit" site the very moment you link to it from the Search Engine!** I can't tell you how often I have spent considerable amounts of time and brain power doing a painstaking search involving multiple keyword phrases, and using more than one Search Engine; just to forget to mark or save the URL address! Often, to find that site again at a later date, I would have to reconstruct my entire search sequence. In NS-Navigator and MS-Explorer you can set an option to maintain a record of all links visited over a period of time, which you can specify. However, these may or may not be all that helpful when you are trying to discern one particular Web page that you looked at three or four weeks ago, from all of the others. On the other hand, once an address is stored in a Browser's Bookmark or Favorites index, one simply has to click on the stored address to return directly to the selected site.

♦ **Always use the most unique keyword phrase to describe what you are looking for.** This will improve the quality of your search and will narrow it down much more quickly than with a loose search criteria. For example if you are looking for a listing of art galleries try using the entire two-word phrase "art galleries" rather than the word "art". Also, take advantage of the "Boolean search" or "refine search" features, whenever you can. In this example, art AND galleries would return a more meaningful result.

♦ **Don't believe everything that you find on the World Wide Web.** Consider the source of the information that you find. If it comes from the official bona fide Site of a known expert or organization, it is most likely valid. However, there is lots of junk out there and one must be discriminating and cross-check if the source is at all questionable. Sometimes it can be very deceiving because people put up very professional looking Web sites that are not the "official" Site for a particular subject. Again, if in doubt, check it out.

♦ **Keep going back for more**. Because of the dynamic and ever-growing nature of the World Wide Web, thousands of new Web sites and Web pages are being added each and every day. Consequently, if you have a particular subject on which you want to keep right up-to-date on the latest information, conduct new searches periodically to find new relevant hits. Also, go back to the original pages that you marked because they are being updated and revised over time. There are also ways to do this automatically through a feature of your Browser called "subscriptions". This option is covered separately in Chapter 7.

Portals To The Web

A new type of "starting point" Web site has emerged on the Internet over the past couple of years. These are called "portals". They offer the user a comprehensive indexed directory service, organized by logical categories and sub-categories that eventually lead to a set of specific Web sites and Web pages as the user clicks deeper down through a series of sequential lists and menus. This method can be more convenient for average Web users because it can often eliminate the need to do a typical Search Engine search from scratch. The idea behind a portal is that there will be sufficient quality content and links to other Web sites that the user will continue to use that particular site as their regular entry point to the rest of the Web. This repeat business generates significant advertising dollars for the portal sponsor.

Competition among portals is now heating up as portal companies compete for users and advertising dollars. Over the last year or so, most of the larger Search Engines have upgraded and redesigned their Web sites and are now calling themselves portals. The competition among portals is so stiff that a number of them are advertising their services and URL on television. To attract users, one portal gives away $10,000 each day to one of its registered users, and offers bigger even cash prizes on certain dates throughout the year.

However, there is no guarantee that the company that owns the "portal" will list all relevant sites. In fact, most of these companies only list Web sites and Web pages that pay to be listed there, either through advertising or by direct payment of fees. Examples of these new custom-designed "portals" can be found at: **www.snap.com** and **www.startingpoint.com.**

Niche Portals For More Focus

Another new development in portals has been the emergence of what are called "niche portals". These are portals at which the content and links are focused on the specific interests of a tiny portion of the general population. They then strive to become the exclusive entry point to the Net for the segment of the population that has common interests with that portal. Accordingly, many industry and special interest group portals are now beginning to appear. For example, there are now specific portals for farmers, job seekers, brides, anglers, seniors, kids, hotels, doctors and police officers, just to name a few. A sample Web site with links to many niche portals is **www.baywalk.com.**

STEP 7 – Saving Your Place On the Web

Mark That Spot

As mentioned in the previous section, looking for information using a Search Engine can be a somewhat time-consuming and laborious task. When you have finally found that special "eureka" site that you have been looking for, it is critical that you mark that address in your Browser right away. This is so that the next time you want to go there, you do not have to go through the entire search process all over again. Both NS-Navigator and MS-Explorer have the capability of marking these sites for you by storing the URL address of the Site. In NS-Navigator these are called Bookmarks and in MS-Explorer they are called Favorites.

NS-Navigator Bookmarks

To record a Bookmark in NS-Navigator, when you are at a Web site or Web page that you would like to mark for future reference, click on the Bookmark button on the toolbar at the top of the Browser window. A drop-down menu will be displayed. Click on Add Bookmark and NS-Navigator will then add the current URL address to its list of saved Bookmark addresses, for later use.

Using the same drop-down menu that displays when you click on Bookmarks, you can also Edit and Delete Bookmarks. These are important features, since after you have spent just a few hours surfing the Web you will most likely find that you have bookmarked many interesting Sites for future visits.

Organizing NS-Navigator Bookmarks

Using the Bookmarks Edit feature, you can create Folders in which to store groups of Bookmarks with a common theme. For example, if you are interested in golf you might want to store the official address of the PGA Tour in a Folder called Golf. With that, you may also want to store the Web site addresses of some of the tour players as well as the addresses of some online golf stores such as **www.callaway.com**. Simply create a Folder called Golf, and then drag and drop the selected Web sites into the Golf Folder using your mouse.

In future sessions, whenever you want to reference a particular Bookmark, simply click on Bookmarks and a list of your Folders will be displayed. Click on the appropriate Folder (e.g. Golf) and the list of saved Web site addresses will then be presented. Simply click on the address you want to link to, and NS-Navigator will take you there directly.

MS-Explorer Favorites

To mark a page as a Favorite for future reference in MS-Explorer go to the Site that you want to mark, and then click on the Favorites button in the upper part of the Browser window. A drop-down menu will appear. Click on Add To Favorites, and MS-Explorer will store the current Web site or Web page address in its Favorites index, for future use.

Organizing MS-Explorer Favorites

Just like with NS-Navigator, you can organize your Favorites into Folders. Marked items can be mouse-dragged from one Folder and dropped into another, the same way that one drags and drops Icons in the computer desktop window. To do this, click in sequence on Favorites/Organize Favorites/New Folder, to create a Golf Folder, for example.

Assuming that you have already been to the appropriate golf sites and marked them, they will appear at the bottom of your list of Folders. Simply drag them and drop them into the Golf Folder.

In future sessions, whenever you want to reference a particular Favorite, simply click on Favorites, and a list of your Folders will be displayed. Click on the appropriate Folder, and the list of saved Web site addresses will then be shown. Simply click on the address you want to link to, and MS-Explorer will take you directly to that Site.

More Advanced Features

Both NS-Navigator and MS-Explorer have additional features that can be used to organize and edit Folders. These include such features as putting Favorites on your desktop (MS-Explorer) or adding individual Bookmarks to the Browser toolbar (NS-Navigator).

However, the features covered in the previous sections are all one really needs to be familiar with to perform basic marking and organizing of Folders. To get a feel for these more advanced capabilities, you can experiment by pointing and clicking on all Bookmarks or Favorites related buttons and menu items in your particular Browser. Things will quickly become obvious.

STEP 8 – Sending and Receiving E-Mail

Probably the most practical and popular feature of the Internet is that it allows users to Send and Receive electronic mail, or E-Mail. Through the Internet, an e-mail message can be sent anywhere in the world as long as it is going to a valid e-mail address. Furthermore, e-mail messages can be sent almost for free because the only direct cost of sending one is paid for as part of your Internet access fee. There are no stamps required, and other postage or long-distance charges don't apply. It is estimated that in 1998 more than 3 trillion e-mails criss-crossed the United States at an average of over 9 billion messages per day!

E-Mail Addresses

A typical e-mail address would be: **username@ispserver.com**. There is always an @ symbol in an e-mail address between the user name and the server name, and the characters are usually, but not always, lower-case characters. This is usually referred to as being "case-sensitive". When entering an e-mail address make sure that you type in *exactly* what was given to you as the address, or it may not work. Watch out for this! If you use a wrong address, you will not know right away. The message will appear to be sent by your Browser and will only he "bounced back" to you hours, or sometimes days, later after it can't be delivered.

E-Mail Programs are Almost Identical

As with Browsers, E-Mail programs are essentially the same, with only minor functional and visual variations from one program to the next. In fact, they are so similar and functionally basic that I won't go into the operational details of any one package here. Figures 6-10 and 6-11 are examples of the e-mail windows of both Netscape Messenger and Microsoft Outlook Mail. Over the years, I have used at least five different e-mail packages and have never had a problem learning how to operate them very quickly just through point and click experimentation.

NS-Navigator and MS-Explorer Both Have E-Mail

Both NS-Navigator and MS-Explorer come packaged with built-in e-mail software programs. There are a number of other e-mail programs available as well. As part of your registration package from your Internet Service Provider, you may even receive yet another e-mail program. To keep things simple, it is recommended that you use the one that is packaged with the Browser that you select since it is totally compatible and will normally be loaded automatically as part of the Browser set-up procedure.

Figure 6-9: Standard E-Mail Features and Functions

E-Mail Data Lines and Button Functions	Description/Remarks
Text Input Lines:	
Send/To line	Enter name and e-mail address of recipient by typing it in or selecting it from your Address Book/List.
Cc. line	Enter e-mail address of anyone who you would like to receive a copy of the message. (optional).
Subject line	Enter a short title that describes the contents of the message.
Text box lines	This is the rectangular box where you type in the text of your message.
Button Functions:	
Compose New Message	This button displays the Compose box that one uses to enter the text of the new message.
Send	This button activates the actual transmission of your current message. Once you have clicked on Send, this message is irretrievably gone unless you are in a special network environment with an Unsend capability.
Attach	This button allows you to attach any file on your computer's disk drive to your outgoing message.
Forward	Allows you to forward a copy of any e-mail you have received to another party.
Route Copies	Allows you to send copies of the current message to a list of recipients as defined by you.
Address Book	Allows you to create an Address List and to access it when you are sending an e-mail so that when you click on a Name on the Address List, it will be inserted automatically into the current message on the appropriate line.
Check Mail	Allows you to check for new mail as long as you are connected to the Internet. This can be made to happen automatically whenever you connect, and at specific time intervals while you are online.

Figure 6-10 – Netscape Messenger – Check Inbox Window

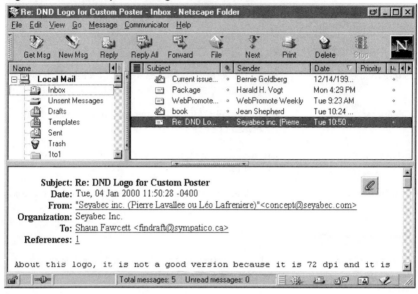

Figure 6-11 – Microsoft Outlook – Compose Mail Window

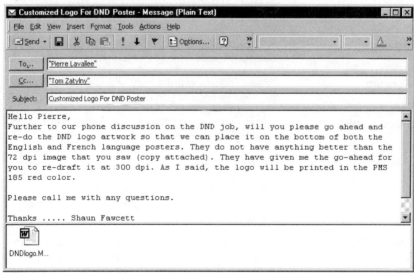

Standard E-Mail Features and Functions

Figure 6-9 contains a list of the standard features of most e-mail programs:

The Address Book feature of most e-mail packages has a number of Edit and Organize features, similar to those available for Bookmarks/Favorites. In addition, there are a number of user-preference Options available in each package. Once again, it is suggested that you spend a bit of time just pointing and clicking to get a feel for all of the specific features of your particular e-mail package.

Tips For Sending E-Mail

Since the Internet was established, a few unofficial, yet imperative, standard protocols have evolved with respect to the sending of e-mails. This norm of online behavior is often referred to as "Netiquette". In addition, this author has learned a few other rules of thumb related to the sending of e-mail. A list of these tips follows:

◆ **Always use a descriptive Subject Line.** There is nothing much more annoying than receiving e-mail in your electronic Inbox with no heading or, a heading that does not explain what the contents of the message is all about. When one receives multiple messages every day, the subject-line is important when reviewing and prioritizing mail that is in one's mail box. Also, if you include a descriptive title as a courtesy, your message is almost guaranteed to be read before ones with blank or meaningless titles.

◆ **Use capital letters sparingly.** The use of all-caps is shunned on the Internet. It is called SHOUTING. Every once in a while a word or two in capitals for particular emphasis is ok, but avoid overdoing it. In addition, cutesy little smiles and similar symbols should be used sparingly. The principle underlying e-mails is clear and concise communication with a minimum of clutter.

◆ **Watch out for "mail rage".** Many an e-mail has been composed and sent when a person was in an angry or upset state. Many people have lived to regret these indiscretions in the cold sober light of the next hour, or the next day. Remember, whenever the Send button has been clicked, your e-mail is gone. If you must compose an e-mail when upset or angry, try not to send it for a couple of hours until things cool down a bit. In any case, it is always a good idea to read an e-mail over carefully at least once before sending it, to make sure you are clearly communicating your message, in a respectful way.

♦ **Opening and Closing Salutations are a nice touch.** Notwithstanding all of its positive aspects, the Internet can be a cold and impersonal place, especially when it comes to sending e-mail. To me there is nothing much colder and more impersonal than receiving an e-mail that doesn't at least say "Hello ....." for the opening, and "Regards ....." or "Thanks ....." or "Take care" at the closing. I think some people have forgotten that this is still interpersonal communication between human beings. No, we can't sign the note anymore with an e-mail, but we can surely personalize it a little bit by at least typing in the recipient's name and then wishing them the best.

♦ **Do not forward junk mail to others.** Sending Junk mail is definitely regarded as an Internet no-no. From time to time, people to whom we have given our e-mail address will have momentary lapses in judgment (yes ... even friends) and will forward what to you is "junk mail". These are often long rambling stories, scraps of wisdom, or collections of joke sheets that are prevalent around the Net. This is the equivalent of opening your regular mail box at home and finding it loaded with unsolicited and unwanted promotional letters and advertising flyers. When you receive one of these in your electronic in-box *do not* forward it on to someone else. Kill it then and there. This kind of unsolicited junk mail is called "spam", and is definitely not acceptable on the Net. If a friend or acquaintance sent it, politely e-mail them back asking if they would please be kind enough to remove your name from their distribution list for that type of item. Explain that you are already inundated with such "spam" mail. Usually, they will get the hint and accommodate you. (You can then refer them to www.spamkillers.com).

♦ **E-Mail can be composed when you are not connected.** Many people don't realize that they don't have to be connected to the Internet when they are composing their e-mails. If an e-mail program is set up properly, e-mail can be composed offline when you are not connected, and the dial-up procedure will be automatically initiated when the Send button is clicked. This means that you don't have to use up valuable connect time or tie up the telephone line unnecessarily when composing e-mail.

♦ **E-Mail is not instantaneous.** When one is finally connected to the Net and starts sending e-mails to all of their online friends, it is natural to think that the very moment the Send button is clicked, the message should go to the intended recipient instantaneously. Not necessarily so. An e-mail is not as reliable as a telephone call when it comes to timely communication! This is because the Internet is a loosely coupled network of telecommunications equipment and computers owned, operated, and managed by many independent companies and government organizations. Your e-mail must often travel through a complex and often circuitous network to get to its destination. For example, if someone schedules maintenance on a computer or a piece of equipment that your e-mail must pass through, your message will be delayed and you won't even know it. If your communication is very urgent, use the standard telephone. Direct voice-to-voice contact over the phone lines is still the only way to be absolutely sure that the message has been received at a particular time.

♦ **Don't forget to check your e-mail regularly.** There is nothing more frustrating than sending an e-mail to someone and them telling you on the telephone a week later that they haven't seen your message because the last time they checked their e-mail was a week ago! If you want people to take your e-mails seriously, make sure that you take theirs seriously too, by checking your Inbox and replying as appropriate at least every couple of days. For example, I make a point of checking my e-mail just about every day.

Receiving E-Mail

This is a very straightforward process. Normally, as soon as your computer is connected to your ISP's computer, any incoming mail will be automatically downloaded to your e-mail program. If the downloading process does not occur automatically, simply click on the Get Mail or Get Message button and any mail will be downloaded immediately. Then it is a simple matter of going to your e-mail program and pointing and clicking as you read and process your messages. After reading a message you can choose to Delete it, or you can drag and drop it into a mail Folder that you have created, for future reference.

It is important to remember that the most common way that computer viruses are spread is through e-mail attachments. As stated earlier in this guide, never open an e-mail attachment if you don't know what it is, or who it came from. Even if you know the sender and you receive an unexpected or suspicious e-mail attachment from that person, it is a good idea to check into it before opening the attachment. Some virus programs have actually attached themselves to outgoing e-mails from infected computers.

Sending E-Mail Attachments

When sending an e-mail it is possible to attach an electronic file to your message. For example, you might want to send someone a copy of a document that you have created in a word processing software package. Or perhaps, you would like to send a photo that you have scanned on a scanner and saved on your computer's hard drive. This is a relatively simple process in both NS-Navigator and MS-Explorer. When in the Compose Mail mode, click on the button that says Attach, or the one that has the Paper Clip symbol on it. This will open a dialogue window that will allow you to browse the files stored on your computer's hard drive. Browse until you locate the file you want to send and then double click on it. It will automatically be attached to your e-mail message when you send it.

Incoming Attachments Can Be a Problem

Sometimes, incoming attachments can cause problems. Normally, to read an attachment you just click on its Icon or graphical symbol that is displayed in your message. In most cases, if the attachment was created using software that also resides on your computer, that program will be loaded automatically and you will be able to view the attachment from that program. In cases where your computer does not recognize the format of the incoming file, it will ask you if you would like to save it somewhere on your hard disk.

It is usually a good idea to save the new file in one of the Folders on your hard disk so that you can later determine its format, and then adjust the appropriate settings in your software to be able to read it. If all else fails and you still cannot read the attachment, send an e-mail to the sender asking them to re-send it in a format that your software can read.

Part 4

Beyond the Basics

7. Other Things You Can Do With the Internet

As stated earlier, the whole purpose of this guide has been to simplify things as much as possible and to stick to the "need-to-know" basics. Consequently, the focus has been on the two primary functions of the Internet that the vast majority of people are interested in; accessing and navigating the World Wide Web, and sending and receiving E-Mail.

However, there are many other things that one can do using the Internet in conjunction with standard Browser software. Some of these can be very useful for the average person who is an occasional user of the Net. Other features may be of more interest to the devoted Webophile. I will list and summarize most of these options briefly here so that readers of this guide will at least be aware of them. Eventually, after becoming fully conversant with the basic functions covered earlier, some people may want to move on, and try a few of these more advanced features.

Electronic Discussion Groups

Over 18,000 Newsgroups

These are known as UseNet Newsgroups. They are a place on the World Wide Web where people can exchange information via electronic messages on topics of particular interest to them. There are over 18,000 Newsgroups on the Web, each one dedicated to a separate topic. With that many topics listed, you can imagine how specialized many of the Newsgroups can be.

Newsgroups are divided into 10 to 15 major categories, each with numerous sub-categories. For example, if you own a 1963 Corvette there is a good chance that there is a specific Newsgroup dedicated to that topic. At that location, people who are interested in 1963 Corvettes (for whatever reason) can exchange information. To find that Newsgroup using your Newsgroup Reader you would go to the Newsgroup called "rec.auto" and scan the various sub-groups until you find the one on 1963 Corvettes. There, you could read messages posted by others, respond to them, as well as post messages of your own.

Special Software and Know-How Required

There is a fair amount of technical know-how involved in accessing and using Newsgroups. There is also a considerable amount of Newsgroup protocol to deal with. For example, a special Newsreader software program is required. NS-Navigator and MS-Explorer both have basic Newsreaders built into them, but the experts recommend the acquisition of a specialized Newsreader such as Free Agent for anyone wanting to get involved in Newsgroups in a serious way. There are entire books, and entire chapters of books, written all about how to access and work with Newsgroups. It is suggested that you consult one of these if the idea of Newsgroups intrigues you.

Newsgroups are Controversial

A final caution on Newsgroups. They are quite controversial these days. Anyone in the world with Internet access can join a Newsgroup. This includes some individuals who might not be quite the upstanding and solid citizens of the world that most of us would like them to be. In other words, Newsgroups abound with kooks and crazies. For example, it is in Newsgroups that people post illegal pornography and hate literature. In addition, many Newsgroups have been essentially "hi-jacked" by special interest groups who flood them with their own propaganda. Also, through Newsgroups one has access to vast amounts of information and "opinions" posted by strangers who may or may not be reliable sources.

Newsgroups Can Be Addictive

Newsgroups are one of the most addictive aspects of the Internet. Many people spend a good part of their day expressing their opinions for the whole world to read using Newsgroups. Nevertheless,

Newsgroups do exist on the Web, and I therefore suggest that if you are interested in them at all, you give them a try. I would do this only after you have become familiar with the basics of the Internet, like surfing the Web and sending/receiving e-mail, as outlined in this guide. When you are ready, a couple of specialized Newsgroup Web sites that you can check out to get a better feel for what they are all about and how they work are: **www.deja.com** and **www.supernews.com**.

Audio and Video Plug-Ins

Plug-Ins are a Netscape-based feature that allow you to extend your Netscape Browser to enable you to hear live and recorded audio programs and to watch video broadcasts over the Internet. Essentially, a Plug-In is a computer program that you can add to your Browser to give it these extra capabilities.

Available Free to Download

These days, there are many Web sites that offer audio and video features. All you need is the Plug-In software to play the audio or video programs. This is not difficult, since just about any Site that offers this type of programming also allows you to download the required software from their Site for free. To do this, you just follow the usually simple download instructions, and within a few moments the appropriate audio or video program will be available on your system. The sponsoring Web sites offer these software Downloads free of charge because they want you to be able to hear or see the products that they are offering by means of audio and/or video presentations. Two popular Netscape Plug-Ins are: RealPlayer for audio and QuickTime for real-time video.

Plug-Ins For Netscape

My suggestion for Plug-Ins is that you wait until you encounter your first Web sites offering the free downloads, at which time you can follow the instructions and they will be installed on your computer thereafter. If you can't wait, and want to know more about these Plug-Ins right away, you can check out the following two Web sites: **www.realplayer.com** and **www.quicktime.com.**

Active X For Microsoft

Microsoft's version of Plug-In's is a technology known as Active X. Although in the end, it will give you about the same capability that Plug-Ins do, it is much more complicated than downloading Plug-Ins. Consequently, I will not get into the details of Active X in this guide. However, there are books available that explain how Active X-controls work, and how to set them up and use them. Two Web sites that will give you more information on Active X are **www.activex.com** and **www.microsoft.com/activex/gallery/ default.htm.**

Live Chat Groups

Similar to Newsgroups in purpose, this is another way to interact with Internet users all over the world, except this time, the interaction occurs in live real-time! Through a number of online "chat services" sponsored by such companies as Yahoo!, one can enter a special interest electronic "chat room" and exchange information and opinions with others gathered in the same room at the same time. Chat rooms are differentiated by topic of interest, similar to how Newsgroups are differentiated.

Special Software Required

As with Newsgroups, special software is required to get involved in online chatting. Plug-Ins are available for Netscape Navigator, and Active X clients are available for Microsoft Explorer. Both types of software can be downloaded from various Web sites. When you access one of the chat sites you can download the appropriate software for free. A few popular chat sites are: **www.ivillage.com, www.talkcity.com, www.yahoo.com, www.pathfinder.com/chat.**

Chat Groups Are Monitored

Chat groups are not as wide open as Newsgroups. Since users normally have to register with the chat service provider, the chat rooms are normally fairly strictly monitored by chat group administrators or monitors. This is to ensure that all group participants respect the usually stringent protocol standards. Since the chats involve live interaction, the chatters can also monitor each other's online behavior. Anyone committing a major breach of protocol can be banned from a chat room and/or from a chat service entirely. However, Chat sites can be as all-consuming as Newsgroups can be, for some users.

Subscribe To and View Pages Offline

With the latest version of MS-Explorer, it is possible to subscribe to your favorite Web sites so that the latest versions of them will be downloaded automatically on a schedule pre-specified by you. Once you have subscribed to a Site, the pages of that site will be automatically downloaded according to the frequency that you have specified. Of course, pages will only download when you are connected to the Web (online). You can also control the parameters of the download in order to economize on storage space and download time.

Many Download Options Are Available

MS-Explorer gives many options for this feature. For example, when subscribing to a Site you can specify a download frequency of, daily, weekly or monthly. You can even choose the hour of the day for the download to take place. Once you have selected Subscriptions, each time you connect to the Web, MS-Explorer will check against your schedule to make sure that the required downloads have taken place. For example, if you specified a download every Wednesday and didn't sign on until Friday, the

Wednesday download would take place at that time. To select the Subscription Option in MS-Explorer, first go to the Site that you want to download. Then you simply click on the Favorites Menu and select Subscriptions.

You Can Control Downloads

MS-Explorer also allows you to specify a number of options to control the extent and impact of automatic subscription downloads. This is an important feature since there are some possible negative aspects to automatic Web page downloading. For example, these downloaded Pages can take up a lot of space on your hard drive. The automatic downloads can also be time-consuming if there are a number of Sites and Pages to download. Accordingly, the download control options allow you to limit the number of pages to download from a Site and to specify the maximum amount of hard drive storage space to use.

In addition, you can choose whether you want to download images, sounds, or videos—all of which use considerable storage space. Finally, you can also select whether to download other pages that are linked to your chosen Page. Whenever you select Subscription mode, you will be presented with dialog windows containing all of these download control options.

Viewing Pages Offline

There are advantages to viewing previously downloaded Pages offline. For example, you don't have to wait for each Page to be downloaded and you view Pages as you wish without worrying about connect time. It also gives you your own custom copy of the Web pages.

As mentioned above, the major disadvantage to downloading Pages for offline viewing is the amount of disk space and download time that it takes. To view Pages that have already been downloaded offline in MS-Explorer, first select the Favorites menu, select Subscriptions, and then choose View All. A dialogue window listing all of the subscribed Pages will be displayed. Click your mouse pointer on the Page or Site that you would like to view.

More Technical Help Is Available

For technical guidance on the foregoing features, there is a pro-liferation of literature in the marketplace, ranging from fairly basic, to technically complex. There are also many specialized books, so keep an eye out for books that focus specifically on your particular area of interest. For example, I once saw a book exclusively about sending and receiving e-mail when using one particular software package. Recently, I ran across a series of books that focus on specific types of business users. For example, the one I remember was titled something like, "The Internet for Sales People."

Part 5

Other Useful Information

8. Some Interesting Internet Sites

To get people started with their Web surfing, here is a short but representative alphabetical list of Web site addresses that should give one a taste for the incredible diversity of information contained on the World Wide Web. Remember, with tens of millions of Web sites out there, this list is only the tiniest little point on the very tip of the iceberg.

Note that all of the following addresses are prefixed by "http://".

A

Aberdeen	www.aberdeen.net.uk
Addictions	www.darc-america.com
Astronauts	www.nasa.gov/index.html
Automobiles	www.autopedia.com
Avalanches	www.avalanche.org

B

Baseball	www.majorleaguebaseball.com
Blood	www.bloodjournal.org
Books	www.amazon.com
Breast Cancer	www.oncolink.upenn.edu/disease/breast
Brides	www.rkbridal.com

C

Canada	www.canada.gc.ca
CIA	www.odci.gov/cia
Computers	www.zdnet.com/pcmag
Cooking	www.cookingindex.com
Crime	www.crime.org

D

Dance	www.ffa.ucalgary.ca/nbc/nbc_main.html
Dentists	www.dental-resources/com
Depression	www.depression.com

Dirt	www.planet.com/dirtweb
Dyslexia	www.bda-dyslexia.org.uk

E

Earthquakes	www.geo.ed.ac.uk/quakes/quakes.html
Education	www.yahoo.com/education
Eggs	www.canadaegg.ca
Emotions	EmotionsAnonymous.org
Eye Care	www.eyetoeyedoc.com

F

Families	www.aifs.org.au
Films	www.mrshowbiz.com/reviews
Football	www.sportserver.com/SportServer/football/
Friendship	www.friendship-force.org
Furniture	www.ikea.com

G

Gardening	www.greengardens.com
Golf	www.pgatour.com
Gorillas	www.kilimanjaro.com/gorilla
Grace	www.cmfellowship.org/backissues/July97/gracepce.htm
Grenoble	www.ville-grenoble.fr/uk/sommaire.html

H

Harvard	www.harvard.edu
Health	www.nih.gov
History	www.lib.virginia.edu
Homes	www.homes-mls.com
Homeopathy	www.homeopathyhome.com

I

Icebergs	www.gov.nf.ca/tourism/adv/iceberg.htm
India	www.india-today.com/itoday
Insomnia	www.sleepbetter.com.au
Insulin	www.insulin-pumpers.org/index.shtml
Intelligence	www.ai.mit.edu/projects/cbcl/web-homepage/web-homepage.htm

J

Jazz	www.radio.cbc.ca/programs/afterhours
Jeep	www.jeep.com
Jet Aircraft	www.boeing.com
Jerusalem	www.jpost.com
Junk	www.winbet.sci.fi/junkyard

K

Kansas	www.state.ks.us
Kangaroos	www.kidsnshoes.com/Kangaroos/ Kangaroosmain.htm
Kites	www.sound.net/~buckchil/kites.html
Knives	www.randallknives.com
Knitting	www.yarns-and.com

L

Librarians	sunsite.berkeley.edu/LibraryLand
Limericks	www.seniors-site.com/poetry/7senses.html
Linguistics	www.engdep1.philo.ulg.ac.bc
Locomotives	www.history.rochester.edu/steam/brown/ index.html
Love	www.percep.demon.co.uk/lovempat.htm

M

Magazines	www.cmpa.ca
Mars	cmex-www.arc.nasa.gov
Medicine	www.nlm.nih.gov
Milky Way	www.jpl.nasa.gov/comet
Music	www.musicmaker.com

N

NATO	www.nato.int
Names	www.babynames.com
Newspapers	www.nytimes.com
Norway	www.uit.no/norge/homepage-no.shtml
Nurses	www.nursingworld.org

O

Olympics	www.sydney.olympic.org

Opera	www.metopera.org
Oprah	www.oprah.com
Origami	www.origami.net
Osteoporosis	www.effo.org

P

Pasta	www.ilovepasta.org
Parenting	www.pathfinder.com/NY1/living/ parenting.html
Pets	www.avma.org/care4pets
Public Relations	www.edelman.com
Presbyterianism	www.freechurch.org/holdfast_4.html

Q

Quakers	www.quaker.org
Quarks	www-ed.fnal.gov/qtoq/collider.html
Queensland	www.queensland-holidays.com.au
Queen Elizabeth	www.royal.gov.uk
Quentin Tarentino	www.blarg.net/~Kbilly

R

Racing	www.formeleins.de
RCMP	www.rcmp-grc.gc.ca
Relaxation	www.behavior.net
Religion	scholar.cc.emory.edu/scripts/AAR/AAR-MENU.htm
Rhubarb	www.rhubarbinfo.com

S

Schizophrenia	www.schizophrenia.com
Seniors	www.unitedseniors.org
Shopping	www.1worldcenter.com
Smithsonian	www.si.edu
Spirituality	www.spiritualityhealth.com

T

Tarantulas	www.nationalgeographic.com/tarantulas/ index.html
Teachers	www.awesomelibrary.org/teacher.html

Teas	www.elixirnet.com
Tobacco	www.tobaccofreekids.org
Transportation	www.iata.org

U

UFO's	www.parascope.com
Ukraine	www.nd.edu/~dknova/uk-emb.htm
Unitarians	www.uua.org
United States	www.state.gov
Universities	www.universities.com

V

Vatican	www.vatican.va
Vegetables	www.veginfo.com
Viagra	www.mensmedicalcenter.com
Virginia	www.state.va.us
Visualization	www.tc.cornell.edu/Visualization/vis.html

W

White House	www.whitehouse.gov/WH
Wines	www.winespectator.com
Wolverines	canadafarnorth.about.com/library/weekly/ aa121099.htm?iam=m
Women	www.womenslinks.com
Worcester	www.valenet.com

X

Xenophobia	www.his-online.de/projects/nation/ index.htm
Xerox	www.xerox.com
X-Files	www.x-files.com
X-rays	www.rs.nic.net.sg/virtuoucity/sata/ pe_xray.htm
Xylophone	www.xylophone.com

Y

Yachts	www.dreamyachts.com
Yale	www.yale.edu
YMCA	www.ymca.int/ymcas.htm

Yorkshire	www.yorkshirenet.co.uk
Yugoslavia	www.gov.yu
Z	
Zamboni	www.zamboni.com
Zen	www.zendo.com
Zirconium	mineral.galleries.com/minerals/silicate/zircon/zircon.htm
Zither	tqd.advanced.org/3588/Renaissance/Town/Music/Zither.html
Zoroastrianism	www.religioustolerance.org/zoroastr.htm

When Addresses No Longer Work

The above addresses were tested and working at the time that this guide was prepared. From time to time, Web sites disappear, or are moved to new addresses. Normally in such cases, when one links to the old address there will be a connecting or forwarding link to the new Site. Don't forget to change your Bookmark or Favorites list when you get to the new one.

If you go to an address and it is no longer valid and there is no forwarding link, you might feel that you are "lost in cyberspace". Not a problem. Just click on the Back button to return to where you started from. To get the new address of the place with the invalid or missing link, you will probably have to go back to your favorite Search Engine and see if you can find it again using the search process.

9. Common Internet Terms

Here are a few common Internet and Internet-related terms that one will invariably encounter at some point when navigating around the World Wide Web using a personal computer. Deliberately, these are the short, plain English definitions.

Baud

This is the unit of measurement used to define the speed at which a modem can transmit and receive data. For example, a 56K modem transfers data at a speed of approximately 56,000 baud.

Browser

A software program used to view information on the Internet. The two most popular Browsers are Netscape Navigator and Microsoft Internet Explorer.

CD-ROM

This is becoming the predominant portable storage medium for electronic information. It is the same size as a music CD and holds over 600 Mbytes of information. Most software programs come on CD-ROM these days.

Cookies

Cookies are small bits of information about you that some Web sites you visit store on your computer. The primary reason for them is so that the next time you visit that particular site you won't have to re-enter all of the registration information.

Cyberspace

A popular term used to describe activities related to the "virtual" world of electronic information technology and communications.

Domain Name

A naming convention used on the Internet to uniquely identify the address of organizations and individuals on the Web. For example: www.nytimes.com.

Download

This is whenever files and or data are transferred electronically from anywhere on the Internet "down" to your computer. The opposite of download is Upload.

E-business

The rapidly growing industry of companies and individuals selling goods and services electronically over the Internet.

E-commerce

The conduct of financial transactions electronically over the Internet such as buying items and paying for them online by credit card.

Encryption

A method of converting the text of an e-mail into a special code that only the sender and receiver can understand. Used as a security measure to protect privacy.

E-mail

The most frequently used service on the Internet that allows users to send electronic messages from their computer to anyone else with an Internet e-mail address.

FAQ

A common term seen around the Internet that stands for Frequently Asked Questions. (see Chapter 11).

FTP

This stands for File Transport Protocol and is the method that is used to download or upload files on the Internet using what are called FTP servers.

Floppy Disk

These are the removable data storage diskettes that one can insert and later remove from the computer. They are usually assigned as "Drive-A" or "Drive-B" on your computer. Also known as the "floppy drive." They are convenient due to their portability, but their storage capacity is limited.

Freeware

This is the name given to software programs available to Internet users that can be downloaded to a personal computer and used free of charge.

Hacker

An expert and often obsessive computer programmer sometimes associated with widely publicized unauthorized intrusions into the computer systems of large companies and governments.

Hard Disk

This is the permanent (i.e. hard) place on your computer where files are copied to and where you retrieve them from after they have been copied. Usually referred to as "C-drive." Hard disks can store huge amounts of data.

Hardware

Any physical piece of equipment that makes up part of your computer system. For example: computer, monitor, modem and printer are all hardware components.

Home Page

The welcome or starting Internet page for any entity with an Internet address.

HTML

Hypertext Markup Language is the programming language used to create electronic pages on the Internet. Also referred to as HTM.

HTTP

Hypertext Transport Protocol is the technical term for the way data files are transferred over the World Wide Web.

Hyperlink

This is the name for the "links" that let you move from place to place within a Web site or from site to site on the Web. Links are normally underlined, highlighted in blue, and sprout a little hand when you move the mouse pointer over them.

Icon

These are the small graphical symbols that one double clicks their mouse on to initiate the operation of a computer software program.

Mbytes

Megabytes are the standard unit for the measurement of computer storage capacity. The capacity of computer memory and disk storage capacity are always measured in terms of Mbytes (MB).

Modem

A circuit board installed in your computer that allows it to send and receive calls via normal telephone lines. Can also be located in a separate box external to your computer.

Netiquette

This term that has been coined to describe appropriate etiquette on the Net, particularly when sending e-mails and conducting other types of online communications. These generally accepted protocols and standards of behavior have evolved over time.

Offline

Refers to when your computer is not connected to the Internet.

Online

The opposite of offline, referring to when your computer is connected by telephone to the Internet.

Portal

A Web site that serves as a comprehensive gateway starting point for the rest of the Wide World Web.

RAM

This stands for Random Access Memory. This is the internal memory of your computer that is used by the various software programs while they are active on your computer.

Search Engine

An Internet Web site where users can enter keywords to help them find the information and/or sites they are looking for.

Server

These are the larger computers that link the typical Internet user's home computer with the rest of the World Wide Web.

Shareware

This is software that is available for download by Internet users that can normally be used free of charge for a limited trial period, after which one can purchase it for ongoing use.

Site

The destination of a unique Internet address and the place where the "content" for an Internet entity is found.(see Web site).

Snail Mail

This term is often used these days to describe regular mail. The obvious inference being that normal mail is very slow compared with e-mail.

Software

This refers to any computer program that runs on your computer. For example; an Operating System such as Windows 98, your Web Browser program, and your E-Mail program, are all software.

Surf

A term used widely to describe the act of a person moving from site-to-site on the Internet via "links" or "hyperlinks".

Toolbar

This term describes a grouping of Buttons displayed in the window of a computer software program, that when clicked or double-clicked by a mouse, activate specific functions of the software. For example, the Toolbars of both NS-Netscape and MS-Explorer appear at the top edges of the windows of those two programs and contain such functions as Back, Forward, Reload, Home, Search, etc. (see Figures 6-6 and 6-7.

URL

The unique Uniform Resource Locator address that is assigned to each site on the World Wide Web. They are always prefixed with "http://www."

Virus

The term used to describe unwanted and destructive computer programs that can seriously damage the software programs that reside on the computers of unsuspecting users. Normally spread by opening suspect e-mail attachments.

Web Site

The destination of a www address where all of the electronic pages of an entity's material are stored. Also referred to as a Site.

Webmaster

This is the individual who is responsible for the design, operation and ongoing maintenance of a Web site.

World Wide Web

Another term for the Internet, and the explanation of the www prefix on all Internet addresses. Also referred to as the Web.

WYSIWYG

This commonly used acronym stands for What You See Is What You Get. For example, when something is WYSIWYG it will appear exactly the same in print as it does on your screen.

10. Nice To Know Information

Every day we are surrounded by numerous references to the Internet. The latest developments and information are tracked in the daily newspaper, Web sites are advertized on radio and television, and billboards display URL addresses. It is difficult to go through an entire day in North America without hearing about e-commerce, e-business, e-trading, e-shopping and e-auctions. References to top Internet-based companies such as amazon.com, e-bay and Yahoo! are becoming commonplace. Information that was once relegated to specialized trade papers has become mainstream in the past two or three years, easily accessible to just about everyone who has even a mild passing interest.

Nevertheless, in spite of all of the information that is now available (or perhaps because there is so much), there are many capabilities the Internet has to offer that many people may not be aware of. The following is a list of a few of these "nice to know" shortcuts and Internet-based services that may be of interest and assistance to the average new user of the Internet.

Notification of Incoming E-mails and Phone Calls

Software programs and telephone services are now available that will alert users to incoming phone calls or e-mails while they are online. For e-mail checking there are a number of programs that you can load onto your computer that will advise you via an on-screen pop-up window and/or audio signal, that you have just received e-mail. Samples of these products can be found at **www.cyber-info.com** and **www.execpc.com/~cnjbrand/ phantom.zip**. For incoming phone call notification, it is best to check with your local phone company to see what they have available or what third-party product they recommend.

You Can Print Web Pages Without Ads

It is possible to print out Web pages without printing the advertisements in both MS-Explorer and NS-Navigator. MS-Explorer has a selective printing capability that will print only the areas highlighted by the user. For NS-Navigator and other Browsers without this selective capability, the solution is to cut and paste the desired parts of the Web page (i.e. without the ads), to a word processing program and then print it out from there.

Be Anonymous On The Net

It is now possible to be completely anonymous on the Internet. A new product called Freedom Software that sells for about USD$50 claims to guarantee users complete anonymity when using the Internet. According to the manufacturer, users get five pseudonyms with the basic software that cannot be linked to one's real world identity. This capability will allow anonymous Web surfing, e-mailing and online chatting. More information on this product is available at **www.freedom.net**.

Junk Mail Can Be Screened Out

Internet junk e-mail (spam) can be significantly reduced by implementing a number of different measures. The most authoritative site on this subject is the Stop Junk E-Mail site at **www.mcs.com/~jcr/junkemail.html**. Some e-mail software programs allow users to set-up filters to reduce Spam. In addition, a number of programs are available that you can install to filter Spam out for you. These include SpamKiller which can be found at **www.spamkiller.com**. There is also a relatively new free Spam-filtering service that claims to be able to eliminate up to 80% of the Spam that you receive. To access this service you supply your name and e-mail address to **www.brightmail.com** and your e-mail will get routed through their server where the Spam will be filtered out.

Music Can Be Downloaded For Free

New technologies are now active on the Internet that allow one to download perfect digital reproductions of music, often for free. This new MP3 technology compresses the digital codes of recorded music into CD files that can be posted on the Internet, e-mailed, and then downloaded to one's home computer. This means that anyone with a CD-ROM writer installed on their computer can create their own personalized music CDs. There are some unresolved copyright issues at stake here so this author will not provide details on exactly how to do this. A little creative Web searching should lead you in the right direction.

Research Your Family Tree Online

Genealogy is becoming a very popular hobby with baby boomers and there is a wealth of family roots information available through the Internet. By far the most notable Web site for this is that of the Mormon Church at **www.familysearch.org**. When the Web site was first introduced it contained about 400 million names and it is expected to reach a total of 1 billion names in 110 countries by the year 2002. Use of the Site is free for everyone, regardless of religious affiliation.

Instant Online Messaging Is Now Available

Instant messaging allows people that are connected to the Internet simultaneously to chat with one another online either one-to-one or in groups, in real-time. It alerts users instantly when a friend comes online or an e-mail is received. Some versions of the software also have fancy features such as real-time stock tickers, up-to-the-minute news headline displays, and e-mails read out loud to the recipient by a synthetic voice. The four most popular instant messengers can be found at: **www.aim.aol.com**, **http://messenger.msn.com**, **http://messenger.yahoo.com**, and **www.icq.com**. Although the technology is impressive, some users are less than enchanted because they say that instant messages are often intrusive interruptions that occur when one is busy doing other things. One also gives up a certain amount of privacy be making it possible for many others to see exactly when they are, or are not, online.

Store Bookmarks and Addresses Online

Bookmarks on the major Web Browsers are well known for their lack of power and flexibility. Basically, they allow one to maintain one-dimensional lists of Web site URL's that have been visited and they offer a few simple editing functions. A smart bookmark program is now being offered free at **www.backflip.com**. This software is smart enough to examine the full text of each page marked and to file a summary of that page in the appropriate category folder as defined by the user. It also keeps a history of all Web sites visited for later reference. Another free service at **www.bungo.com** allows users to store their personal information such as calendars, bookmarks, personal notes, addresses and phone numbers online on the Web for easy access from anywhere. It also allows users to publish reading lists to share with others. Online chats and instant messaging are also possible.

Although these services are convenient, useful and free, some users have expressed concerns about security and privacy with so much personal information stored at a privately-owned site on the Web.

Get Online Help With Web Searches

The goal of a new Web search helper service is to get customers to their desired Web sites within 7 minutes. This service was set up because surveys have revealed that as many as 65% of Web searches go unsatisfied. Evidently, this is because most of the major search engines return so many potential sites (usually thousands) that users have trouble finding what they are looking for. The service is not free. It costs USD$ 9.99 per month or $0.99 per search. The company, which can be found at

www.webhelp.com actually uses people who are search experts to conduct the searches on the customer's behalf.

Have Your Own Personalized Clipping Service

For those who may not know, a clipping service provides a person or a company with copies and/or summaries of all media coverage that the person or company receives. There are a number of companies that offer similar services on the Internet. To use these free services you simply define specific names and/or keywords that you want information on and the service will scan all of its sources on a daily basis for mentions according to your pre-defined criteria. Most of these services will send you e-mail with a hyperlink connecting you to the source of the mention whenever they find a "hit". Be careful with these e-mail clipping services because they can fill up your in-box very quickly. One service that avoids e-mails (Excite) posts all of its matches to a custom Web page that you can visit at your convenience. Some of the most notable of these online clipping services are: **http://alerts.yahoo.com** (general), **www.companysleuth.com** (corporate intelligence), **www.infonautics.com** (sports, general), and **http://nt.excite.com** (general). For anyone conducting research or just wanting to keep up-to-date on a particular topic, these are very powerful tools.

With the incredible amount and diversity of information on the Internet these days, it is essential to have tools and shortcuts such as the foregoing to help one sort through the vast information stockpile.

11. Frequently Asked Questions

"Do I really need to get connected to the Internet?"
No, not if you don't want to. It is always your choice. On the other hand, if you are at all interested in staying in direct touch with how the world is evolving when it comes to information dissemination and communications, as we begin the new millennium, the Internet is definitely the way to go.

One doesn't have to be an expert to realize that something very big is happening with this Internet thing these days, and it is gaining momentum. Just pick up a newspaper, or tune in to a radio or television station and try to go for fifteen minutes without a mention of the Net. For that matter, try to find a company these days that does not have a Web site and an e-mail address.

Let's face it, the Internet is here to stay and here to grow. Just imagine the beginning of the telephone era in the early 20th Century, or the advent of the television in the early 1950's, and consider their impact on our lives. That's what is happening now with the Internet, except in a much more compressed timeframe due to the rapid pace of technological change today. Internet access is almost becoming mandatory now for kids and students at all levels, if they want to be successful in their studies. If you are a parent or grand parent, being Internet-friendly is quickly becoming an important part of understanding and communicating with the younger generation; not to mention, communicating with your friends around the world via e-mail.

Today, access to the Internet can improve the quality of your life. For example, from your own home with just a few clicks of the mouse you can: do your banking, check out the value of your investments, price and buy a new car, check your lottery ticket, book a vacation, conduct research on your family tree, order books or music CD's, do your grocery shopping, view the new houses-for-sale listings, send e-mail to almost anywhere in the world; and the list goes on and on. This kind of direct, instant, and convenient access to information empowers individuals in modern society in a way that they have never been empowered before. All of a sudden, in the last few years the playing field just got significantly more level for many millions of people.

No, you don't have to get connected, but if you choose not to, it is now fair to say that the very quality of your life may well suffer due to your limited access to the most powerful information and communication tool of the new millennium.

"What's the difference between the Internet and the World Wide Web?"

Although the two terms are frequently used interchangeably, they are not exactly the same thing. The World Wide Web is actually a sub-component of the Internet. The other components also embraced by the Internet are: File Transfer Protocol (FTP), E-Mail, UseNet, and Chat services. The World Wide Web is actually the newest component of the Internet and by far the most popular. This is largely due to its multi-media mix of graphics, text, animation, and sounds, all of which appeal to a wide cross-section of individual and corporate users. (see page 33).

"Do I need a separate telephone line for the Internet?"

No, a separate telephone line is not required for Internet access. However, unless you have high-speed service, when your phone line is being used for the Internet it is tied-up just like with a regular phone call, and is therefore not available for other communications such as voice and fax. Depending on your level of usage and the needs of others you live or work with, you may decide, or be forced, to order a separate line. (see page 49).

"How much does it cost to get onto the Internet?"

Not that much if you are just talking about telephone access to the Net. Anywhere from $9 or $10 per month for minimum access hours (e.g. 7 to 10 connect hours per month), to $29.95 per month for unlimited online connect time. Of course, this assumes that you already have the computer hardware and software that is needed before making the connection. If you also need to buy the basic equipment, you can add another $1,000 to $1,500 for a desktop PC and a modem with appropriate software. (see pages 47-50).

However, with the advent of Internet appliances such as WebTV and iPhones it is now possible to access the Web and perform basic e-mailing and browsing functions without a computer. These devices range in price between USD$100 and $500, and monthly Internet access charges still apply. (see page 48).

"Is there a central "phone book" of e-mail addresses?"
No, there is no such directory that contains all e-mail addresses. And it is not likely that there ever will be. This is due to the fundamental nature of the Internet as a loosely coupled network of computers dispersed around the globe with no central registration or control over who does, and who does not, have access to the Net. However, there are a number of online telephone directories that do list e-mail addresses when they manage to get that information. (see page 123).

Probably the best you can do for your own records is to compile your own personal index of Favorites/Bookmarks in your Browser or using an online service to cover Web sites. For e-mail addresses of friends, acquaintances and business contacts you can use your e-mail software's Address Book or an online service. (see pages 74-78).

"What are "cookies", and are they a threat to my personal privacy?"
That all depends on how you interpret the purpose and use of cookies. Cookies are small bits of information about you that some Web sites you visit store on your computer. The primary reason for creating cookies is so that the next time you visit that particular site you won't have to re-enter all of the registration information. A cookie record is only readable by the company that

created it and they cannot obtain more information about you than you have personally given to them. Some people have no problem with cookies and others regard them as a gross invasion of privacy. Both Netscape Navigator and Internet Explorer allow users to disable cookies if they want to. To set cookie options in Netscape Navigator click on Edit/Preferences/Advanced and a dialogue box will be displayed giving you options to control cookies. To do this in Internet Explorer click on View/Internet/Options to display the cookie options.

Remember; once you have disabled cookies you may find yourself having to re-enter data quite often when you return to sites, and you may have problems interacting with some Web sites.

"Can other people read my e-mail without me knowing it?"
Not normally. Unless of course, some genius "hacker" who has already cracked the codes for the Pentagon computer network should want to steal a look at your e-mail. This is a highly unlikely eventuality for most of us. We just aren't that important. Suffice it to say, anything is remotely possible, but someone getting into your mailbox deliberately is extremely unlikely. Your odds might be better in the Lottery. If you are really worried about very sensitive e-mails, both MS-Explorer and NS-Navigator provide an encryption capability in their compose e-mail functions.

"Do I need any special equipment to access the Internet?"
Yes, either a fully operating personal computer with a modem and certain required software programs, or one of the new Internet appliances. (see page 48). For a computer, special modem software will be supplied and loaded onto your computer when your modem is installed. In addition to that, to access and/or "surf" the World Wide Web you will need a Browser program such as Netscape Navigator or Microsoft Explorer.

Finally, for e-mail you will need an e-mail program. Both MS-Explorer and NS-Netscape come with built-in e-mail programs, although there are a number of others available on the market.

For the sake of simplicity and compatibility, it is recommended that you use the one supplied and loaded with your Browser program. See pages 47 to 52 for a more complete explanation of equipment requirements.

"Can I get an e-mail back after sending it in error?"

Not normally. In almost all cases, if you are connected to the Internet when you click on the Send button, that e-mail is on its way into cyberspace via your ISP's computer. This is why it is important to review e-mails and think about them carefully before touching the Send button, in order to make sure that your e-mail is clearly communicating the intended message. See pages 38 and 79 for more discussion of the pitfalls of sending e-mails too quickly.

The only possible exceptions to this are certain "controlled" environments such as company Intranets that use what are called "groupware" software tools. Some of these may have an "unsend" capability for use when one wants to retrieve an e-mail during the same online session. Even with these, after the end of the current session the messages would normally be irretrievable.

"Can e-mails give my computer a virus?"

Yes, e-mail attachments are the primary way that computer viruses are transferred on the Internet. However, there is no need to get paranoid about this possibility. Although computer viruses do exist, they have been "hyped" way out of proportion by the media. To protect against possible viruses one needs to be careful about suspicious e-mails they receive with attachments. If seriously in doubt about an unsolicited e-mail from an unknown sender, delete it before ever opening it. If you don't want to do that, you will either have to take a chance and open it, or you can get an expert, such as a "tekkie" at your local computer store to take a closer look at it. You can also get virus scanning software that can determine if there is a known virus present.

Don't forget, it is also possible to contract a virus while download-ing files from the Web to your computer. If in doubt about whether to download from a suspicious and/or unknown site, check it out through friends or professionals for their advice on whether to chance it. Otherwise, you do it at your own risk. For more information on viruses, and virus detection and protection, including some free downloads, an extensive Site can be found at: **www.commandcom.com**.

"Can people steal my credit card number if I shop online?"
Yes, it is supposedly technically possible for someone to gain access to your credit card number as you transfer it over the Web. However, all reputable companies who do e-commerce over the Net use state-of-the-art encryption security software.

This author has never actually heard or read about an actual documented case of a credit card number being misappropriated via the Internet. This is another one that has been blown way out of proportion by the media. Yes it is possible, but at the same time, the security measures at reputable Web sites are likely better than they are at most businesses to which many of us al-ready give our credit card numbers over the telephone. At least the Web sites use encryption techniques to protect us. For ex-ample, I sometimes order flowers by telephone and pay for them by giving my credit card number over the phone line. As far as I know, there are no encryption programs or any other measures used by the florist or by the telephone company to ensure that my card number is not misused.

Most of us will remember when bank machines came online a decade or so ago. At the time, many people, again fueled by un-balanced media coverage, were worried about their money some-how disappearing electronically between the machine and their bank account. Of course that never happened, and bank machines are now a dependable part of the everyday lives of most of us.

"Is the Internet safe for my kids and/or grand kids?"

Yes it should be, with some qualifications. The World Wide Web should be a safe place for kids if proper software controls and parental supervision are in-place. The Internet is simply a microcosm of modern multi-cultural civilization. It spans the positive aspects of society, as well as, many of society's negative sides.

As far as this author is concerned, the Internet has not been responsible for introducing anything negative that was not already "out there" in the big bad world. The big difference is that, because of its technology and reach, the Net has made both the good and the bad much more directly accessible to everyone, including children. And as we know, children are very curious and their sense of judgment isn't necessarily fully developed. Because of this, if unchecked they can end up going to places on the Internet that are less than healthy.

To protect against your children or grandchildren going places on the Net with undesirable content, a number of child protection and security software programs are readily available. Some of them block out certain known unsavory sites, and others screen and filter out sites based on certain key words that are found there. These programs can be purchased online on the Net or in computer stores at a very reasonable cost. However, these days many reputable ISP's now supply this software free as a public service and they often include it as a value-added item, as part of a family Internet sign-up package. One of the most well-known of these products can be found at www.netnanny.com. In addition, there are a number of very informative Web sites with excellent information on measures that can be taken to protect kids. These Sites include: **www.yahooligans.com, www.safekids.com,** and **www.fbi.gov/library/pguide/pguide.htm.**

Nevertheless, no matter how good this child protection software may be, it will never substitute for proper parental supervision. In particular, if your child or grandchild is spending inordinate amounts of time in Chat groups, make it a point to find out what is going on, and take parental regulatory action if warranted, in exactly the same way you would if you found them "hanging" with the wrong crowd at school.

"Can I have my own Internet Web page?"

Absolutely! In fact, there are many Sites on the Web that offer a free Home Page service. Probably the most well known place to create your own free Web page is at **www.geocities.com**. Increasingly, the larger Internet Service Providers and major portals are offering users the ability to create their own personal online Home pages.

Another free Web page service that is very user friendly, is offered by a Chat group called TalkCity at **www.talkcity.com**. They virtually hold your hand through the process, and then even allow you to upload a photograph of yourself to post on your Web page. The really neat thing about Web pages is that, once your Page is created, it doesn't matter on which computer it actually resides, since your unique URL address will be accessible from anywhere else on the World Wide Web.

Of course, if you feel technically inclined, you can also create your own Web page or Web site from scratch using the HTML language with some special Web page creation software programs, such as Homesite or Hot Dog. Quite often, when you sign-on with an ISP company, their package will include some space on their server for your own Web page to reside at no extra charge.

User friendly Web publishing tools are now available that allow one to create a basic Home Page without even knowing HTML. With these, you can simply use the "drag and drop" method to design and publish your own home page. Some Web sites where these programs can be found are: **http://webattack.com/ shareware/webpublish**, **www.bigplanet.com/dwp** and **www.biznizweb.com/tsi**.

Finally, there are thousands of Web page designing and building professionals (and amateurs) out there who are quite willing to create a Web page for you, for a fee. For a simple Web site, comprising a page or two, plus a couple of photos or graphics to upload, this can be quite inexpensive, and is worth checking into if you want a customized Site with a professional look. Just consult the Yellow Pages under Internet, or try your Search Engine to find these people. It may be best to look for someone in your local area if you want to be able to meet face-to-face and don't want to be bothered with the technicalities of transferring electronic files back and forth from computer to computer. In my area there are a couple of kids who have a stall at a local mall where they will create a simple personal Web page, including a photo, for $21.95.

"Can I have access to my e-mail via the Internet when I travel?"

Yes, it is possible to access your e-mail whenever you travel. The easiest way is to take a laptop computer on your trip that is set up with the appropriate software needed to access the Internet. To access the Net from your away-from-home location it will be most cost-effective if you have a local number that you can dial from that place for toll-free access to your ISP and your e-mail account. Many of the larger companies offer local dial-up access in many cities around the world. Some of these larger ISP companies include Compuserve, AT&T, Microsoft and IBM.

The best approach would be to set-up an account with the ISP that you choose, before your trip. Then you can set-up your software and test it so that there will be no surprises at your destination. Of course, it is possible to access your regular e-mail account from abroad without local dial-up capability if you are willing to pay the long-distance charges for dialing your home area code. If you travel infrequently and just want to check your e-mail occasionally while en route, paying a few long distance charges may be cheaper and less trouble than setting up an account with a new service provider.

If you subscribe to one of the free online e-mail services such as hotmail.com all you need is local access to the Web where ever you happen to be, and then you can directly access the hotmail Web site to read and send your e-mails.

"How can I be certain that someone received my e-mail?"
The only way to be absolutely sure if someone received e-mail you sent to pick up the phone and ask them. Message receipt confirmation is not yet standardized on all e-mail software used on the Internet. Even if your software has this feature and you have it enabled properly, it will only work when communicating with another e-mailer who has the same feature enabled, and when their ISP is set-up to send receipts. As stated earlier in this guide it is incorrect to assume that intended recipients receive their e-mail instantaneously, or even at all sometimes. When ISP's are changing over to new servers or making other network changes, e-mails are often known to disappear mysteriously into cyberspace.

"Can I find someone's telephone number and mailing address on the Internet?"
There are a number of sites that offer online directory services including telephone numbers and mailing addresses. In some cases they even list e-mail addresses, when they have them. The Web site **www.teldir.com** contains a comprehensive set of links to telephone directories around the world. This one-stop-site links to directories that cover more than 150 countries. In five languages, it lists white pages, yellow pages, business listings, fax numbers and e-mail addresses (when available). One shouldn't have to look further than this.

"What happens to my privacy when I provide my personal coordinates while making an online purchase or registering for an online service?"
Depending on where you register, it is possible that your personal privacy could be compromised. Today, most reputable companies have a published Privacy Policy statement available on their Web site that will tell you exactly what they will and will not do with

the personal information that you supply to them. If you have concerns about a particular situation make sure you read that Site's policy statement before divulging your personal information. If a Site requests personal contact information and it does not publish a privacy policy, you will be giving it the information at your own risk. These days it would not be unreasonable to refuse to do online business with Sites that do not publish a privacy policy.

Index

Index

About the Author

Shaun Fawcett studied business administration, majoring in electronic data processing, at community college in the 1970's. He then spent the first ten years of his career as a computer programmer and systems analyst. Not wanting to remain a "tekkie" for the rest of his life, in the early 1980s he shifted his career path to that of a "'generalist".

In that role, he worked for a number of years as a management consultant, doing everything from designing and implementing national computer systems, to acting as the primary co-author of a major airport master plan. As time passed, he lost touch with his technical computer roots and eventually became just another "dumb user" in the era of the PC. During that period, he was a key player in the start-up phases of three government organizations and one international institute, and he also managed to do some part-time business consulting.

In the mid 1990's Shaun went back to school and obtained his Master of Business Administration from the University of Ottawa. While working on his M.B.A. he was essentially forced to once again become "computer friendly" via the Internet, which was at that time in its early days as an information network for the general public.

After completing his M.B.A. in 1996, Shaun moved to Montreal to work as a marketing executive with an international training institute. Then in 1998, he formed his own business communications and consulting firm in that city. Shaun's personal experiences with the Internet over a number of years, coupled with his observations on many people's hesitancy to embrace computer technology in general, are what prompted him to develop this guidebook to the Internet for the ordinary person.

Internet Basics *without fear!*

Order Form

Phone Orders:	1-800-600-6550 (Toll Free)
Fax Orders:	(514) 989-7283
E-mail Orders:	findraft@sympatico.ca
Postal Orders:	Final Draft Publications
	1501 Notre-Dame West
	Suite No. 5
	Montreal, Quebec, Canada
	H3C 1L2

Please Send: _____ copies of Internet Basics *without fear!* to:

Person Ordering:_____

Company Name: _____

Street Address: _____

City: _____ State/Prov.: _____

Zip/Postal Code:_____

Telephone No.: (___)_____ E-mail: _____

Basic Order:

A: No. of copies: _____ (as per above)

B: Cost Per Copy: $_____ (CAN $17.95; USA $12.95)

C: Total Base Cost: $_____ (C = A x B)

Taxes:

D: GST at 7%: $_____ (D = C x .07 ; Canada only)

Shipping:

E: $4.00 per book: $_____ (E = A x $4. ; postage, packaging)

Total Of Order: $_____ **(Total = C+D+E)**

Payment: GST No. 142639426

❏ Cheque enclosed.   ❏ Money Order enclosed.

❏ Payment by **VISA** Credit Card:

Credit Card Number: _____ Exp. Date: ___/___

Cardholder Name: _____

Cardholder Signature: _____

Call Toll Free and Order Now!

Internet Basics *without fear!*

Order Form

Phone Orders:	1-800-600-6550 (Toll Free)
Fax Orders:	(514) 989-7283
E-mail Orders:	findraft@sympatico.ca
Postal Orders:	Final Draft Publications
	1501 Notre-Dame West
	Suite No. 5
	Montreal, Quebec, Canada
	H3C 1L2

Please Send: _____ copies of Internet Basics *without fear!* to:

Person Ordering:_____

Company Name: _____

Street Address: _____

City: _____ State/Prov.: _____

Zip/Postal Code:_____

Telephone No.: (___)_____ E-mail: _____

Basic Order:

A: No. of copies: _____ (as per above)

B: Cost Per Copy: $_____ (CAN $17.95; USA $12.95)

C: Total Base Cost: $_____ (C = A x B)

Taxes:

D: GST at 7%: $_____ (D = C x .07 ; Canada only)

Shipping:

E: $4.00 per book: $_____ (E = A x $4. ; postage, packaging)

Total Of Order: $_____ (Total = C+D+E)

Payment: GST No. 142639426

❏ Cheque enclosed. ❏ Money Order enclosed.

❏ Payment by **VISA** Credit Card:

Credit Card Number: _____ Exp. Date: ___/___

Cardholder Name: _____

Cardholder Signature: _____

Call Toll Free and Order Now!

Internet Basics *without fear!*

Order Form

Phone Orders:	1-800-600-6550 (Toll Free)
Fax Orders:	(514) 989-7283
E-mail Orders:	findraft@sympatico.ca
Postal Orders:	Final Draft Publications
	1501 Notre-Dame West
	Suite No. 5
	Montreal, Quebec, Canada
	H3C 1L2

Please Send: _____ copies of Internet Basics *without fear!* to:

Person Ordering:_____
Company Name: _____
Street Address: _____
City: _____ State/Prov.: _____
Zip/Postal Code:_____
Telephone No.: (___)_____ E-mail: _____

Basic Order:
A: No. of copies: _____ (as per above)
B: Cost Per Copy: $_____ (CAN $17.95; USA $12.95)
C: Total Base Cost: $_____ (C = A x B)
Taxes:
D: GST at 7%: $_____ (D = C x .07 ; Canada only)
Shipping:
E: $4.00 per book: $_____ (E = A x $4. ; postage, packaging)

Total Of Order: $_____ **(Total = C+D+E)**

Payment: GST No. 142639426
❏ Cheque enclosed. ❏ Money Order enclosed.
❏ Payment by **VISA** Credit Card:
Credit Card Number: _____ Exp. Date: ___/___
Cardholder Name: _____
Cardholder Signature: _____

Call Toll Free and Order Now!